Ryszard Kapuściński: Reportage and Ethics
or Fading Tyranny of the Narrative

Polish Studies -
Transdisciplinary Perspectives

Edited by Krzysztof Zajas / Jaroslaw Fazan

Volume 2

PETER LANG
Frankfurt am Main · Berlin · Bern · Bruxelles · New York · Oxford · Warszawa · Wien

Kinga Kosmala

Ryszard Kapuściński: Reportage and Ethics or Fading Tyranny of the Narrative

PETER LANG
Internationaler Verlag der Wissenschaften

Bibliographic Information published by the Deutsche Nationalbibliothek
The Deutsche Nationalbibliothek lists this publication in the Deutsche Nationalbibliografie; detailed bibliographic data is available in the internet at http://dnb.d-nb.de.

Cover Design:
© Olaf Gloeckler, Atelier Platen, Friedberg

ISSN 2191-3293
ISBN 978-3-631-61848-6
© Peter Lang GmbH
Internationaler Verlag der Wissenschaften
Frankfurt am Main 2012
All rights reserved.

All parts of this publication are protected by copyright. Any utilisation outside the strict limits of the copyright law, without the permission of the publisher, is forbidden and liable to prosecution. This applies in particular to reproductions, translations, microfilming, and storage and processing in electronic retrieval systems.

www.peterlang.de

To my Mother

The prudent mariner will not rely solely on any single aid to navigation.

–an old sailing maxim

Contents

Acknowledgments 11

Part One
INTRODUCTION

I. Life and Oeuvre 15
II. Reportage – Historical Overview and Theory 24
III. Constant Negotiation 36

Part Two
TYRANNY

I. The Useful Discord 41
II. Characters vs. Discourse 50
III. Power 55
IV. The Narrator 59
V. The End (or lack thereof) 64

Part Three
TRAUMA

I. Unfathomable *Imperium* 69
II. Trauma and Its Consequences 72
III. Structure 75
IV. (No) Resolution 87

Part Four
TALES

I. Reportage from the Self 91
II. Traveling with the Father of History 94
III. Approaching the Unknown 98
IV. Egalitarianism 111
V. Self-critique 115

Part Five
ETHICS

I. Ideological Ethics 121
II. Conclusion 129

Works cited 131

Acknowledgments

I would like to offer my warmest thanks to Bożena Shallcross for her outstanding help and excellent advice in all the stages in writing my book. Also, I would like to thank my mother and the rest of my family for their help and unwavering faith in me.

I owe very special thanks and expressions of gratitude to The Maria Kuncewicz Fund, the Council of Educators in Polonia, and The Kosciuszko Foundation (The American Center of Polish Culture, Promoting Educational and Cultural Exchanges and Relations Between the United States and Poland since 1925) for granting me publication scholarships and making publishing this book possible.

Part One
INTRODUCTION

I. Life and oeuvre

Ryszard Kapuściński's life and oeuvre are a testament to the need of participation in history as it unfolds, history *in statu nascendi*. Kapuściński, one of the leading figures in Polish reportage, was born in 1932 in Pińsk (present-day Belarus, at that time a part of Poland) and died in January 2007 in Warsaw. He was an active proponent of establishing the communist system in post-war Poland, a member of Związek Młodzieży Polskiej (Union of Polish Youth) in the 1950s as well as of Polska Zjednoczona Partia Robotnicza (The Polish United Workers' Party) between 1953 and 1984, a direct witness to the creation of and collapse of independent African states in the 1960s and 1970s, the guerilla movements against military regimes in South America, the military combat in Honduras and El Salvador, the coup in Angola, the 1974 revolution in Ethiopia, the anti-Shah revolt in Iran, the 1980 strike in the Gdańsk Shipyard, and ultimately the collapse of the Soviet empire in 1991.

Kapuściński's oeuvre is extraordinary. Putting aside obvious elements such as the incredible variety of topics or the vast number of places he visited and described, the sheer diversity of genres in his work is impressive: lyrical poetry, newspaper articles and reports, war correspondences, reportage books, philosophical reflections, memoirs, interviews, and even photography. The size and duration themselves are astonishing; he debuted as a poet in 1951 and remained an active writer until his death in 2007.

In *Lapidaria I* Kapuściński explains "[I] became a foreign correspondent in 1956, at the age of 24. Since then I have worked in this profession continuously, specializing in the problems of underdeveloped countries, particularly in Africa, Asia and Latin America" (208). Kapuściński's numerous travels in this capacity resulted in a diverse body of work consisting of variegated literary genres. This book concentrates on his book-length reportage works, products of the author's travels to distant lands, regarded by some as exempla of mastery in the reportage genre and by others as ethically questionable semi-fictional stories. The book's intention is to look closely at the process of the aesthetic formation of the author's travel experiences into book-length texts and the ideological paradigm shaping his representation of the facts. In addition to that, the effects of authorial re-shaping of documentary material, the question of authenticity or fabrication thereof, and the epistemological responsibility of a reportage writer are also examined. The objective of this book is neither an analysis of Kapuściński's entire oeuvre, nor his exhaustive biography, as these goals have already been achieved by other scholars. Hence, only four Kapuściński's crucial works are this book's focus.

1. Structure of the study

Part 2 of this book, immediately following this Introduction, focuses on the analysis of *The Emperor: Downfall of an Autocrat (Cesarz)*.[1] The first of Kapuściński's books translated into English, *The Emperor*, recounts the collapse of Haile Selassie's over 40-year long tyranny in Ethiopia in 1974. The book is an excellent study of the problems and tragedies a lonely yet opportunistic individual encounters when irrevocably entangled in the web of a totalitarian system. The book's main narrative describes the conflict of two worlds, each world expressed through the use of its own language. The conflict is intriguingly articulated through the dynamic interplay of two idioms: that of the emperor's courtiers living in resplendent luxury juxtaposed with the rest of society fighting extreme poverty and starvation. *The Emperor*, the ninth of Kapuściński's reportage books, is his most widely known and his most ideological 'African' book. While the events of the main narrative take place in Africa and detail only one of many coups d'etat Kapuściński witnessed, the observations and reflections cannot be more universally poignant.

Part 3 focuses on Kapuściński's 'Russian' book, *Imperium*.[2] Situating his work mostly during the Soviet Union's last years, the author encapsulates in this narrative his life-long contention with one of Poland's most infamous Others, namely Russia/Soviet Union. *Imperium* is a result of Kapuściński's many journeys through the Soviet Union, the last one during the final years of the Soviet Union's existence (1989-1991); the book is a fascinating glimpse at the final moments of the once immortal and invincible empire. Notably, Kapuściński starts the book with his childhood memories of hunger and fear caused by the Soviet invasion of Poland in September of 1939. *Imperium* then opens with personal and vivid descriptions of childhood horror. In the 'Russian' book, the author tries to recapitulate his multifarious encounters with Russia but finds it impossible to enclose Russia in any kind of delimiting structure, as the topic is both intimate and disconcerting for Kapuściński. His typical method of employing the point of view of a seemingly gullible and trusting wanderer is much more apparent in this book. Moreover, even the style sets *Imperium* apart from his 'African' and 'South American' books; *Imperium*'s narration is very slow, with its long sentences paralleling the great Russian ex-

---

1 First Polish edition – Warszawa: Czytelnik, 1978. English translation by William R. Brand, Katarzyna Mroczkowska-Brand, New York; London: Harcourt Brace Jovanovich, 1982.
2 First Polish edition – Warszawa: Czytelnik, 1993. English translation by Klara Glowczewska, New York: A. A. Knopf, 1994.

panses. The unhurried stories and lack of rigid structure also mirror the crumbling of the former empire.

Part 4 examines two works, *Lapidaria* and *Travels with Herodotus*. *Lapidaria* is essentially a pastiche of writings by Kapuściński, culled from several decades. It originally appeared as six separate volumes, the first of which was published in 1990, the last (sixth) in 2007.[3] *Lapidaria* differs significantly in form and poetics from the earlier works, as in this book the author turns inward to undertake a journey of self-reflection. The texts gathered in this book are primarily literary vignettes, often containing only a few sentences. They include observations of the contemporary world, reflections on our civilization at the turn of the millennia, notes remembered from the author's several decades of travel, and, perhaps most interestingly, observations about Kapuściński's own writing process and experience as a journalist. The second book analyzed in Part 4 is *Travels with Herodotus*, published in Poland in 2004.[4] The book is Kapuściński's literary summary of his life-long travels to the farthest corners of the world, as well as – with a dubious degree of self-awareness – his valediction to writing. *Travels with Herodotus* is an extensive report and a colorful tale from Kapuściński's inaugural journeys to foreign lands and the awakening of his reportorial sensitivity to otherness. In *Travels*, he also crosses the borders of time and space, with the narration happening simultaneously on several temporal and spatial planes. The accounts of his first several foreign reporting trips are interwoven with fragments from *The Histories* by Herodotus, which Kapuściński (supposedly) had in tow throughout his entire professional life. As Kapuściński reads *The Histories* over and over again, Herodotus' experiences become a significant paradigm for construing reality for the author of *Travels*. And not just that, for Kapuściński Herodotus becomes the personification of the spirit of Dichtung.

The concluding chapter contains my closing observations on Kapuściński's treatment of narrative, ideology, and ethics, and problems encountered throughout the study.

In my opinion, *The Emperor*, *Imperium*, *Lapidaria*, and *Travels with Herodotus* – analyzed in this book in chronological order – not only possess exceptional literary significance but also frame Kapuściński's reportage writing career with salience and precision.[5] All four books represent milestones of his writing

---

3   First part of the series was published in 1990; the last, sixth one came out in 2007. All six parts of the series were published by Czytelnik in Warszawa, none of it have been translated into English.
4   First Polish edition – *Podróże z Herodotem*, Kraków: Znak, 2003. English translation by Klara Glowczewska, Vintage International, New York, 2008.
5   *The Emperor*, *Imperium* and *Travels with Herodotus* have been translated into English. As of now, I am not aware of any attempts to translate *Lapidaria* into English.

career and showcase the transformation of his treatment of narrative, method, and style, which are accompanied by significant changes in the author's philosophy of life and his Weltanschauung.

I have chosen to analyze Ryszard Kapuściński's reportage works, or specifically to concentrate on the ethical component of his version of reporting factual events, because it encompasses what I see as a fundamental issue in the stance and mission of today's literature as well as mass media – the question of epistemological responsibility.

Although there are several more books by Kapuściński known in the English literary world worth mentioning, structural constraints preclude their inclusion in this study. These books, similar to the ones I analyze in this book, serve to establish the author's place in the tradition of reportage and contain descriptions of the author's continuous attempts at participating in the challenging lives of the communities he describes. Among many other important books by Kapuściński is *Another Day of Life*.[6] It is a volume based on the author's African experiences concentrating on the end of Portuguese rule in Angola. Chaotic, ruthless, and unpredictable fighting in one of the world's then politically hottest spots causes most of the foreigners to leave Angola in panic. The author describes not necessarily the actual combat and warfare or the opposing sides of the conflict but rather the overwhelming mood of uncertainty, disorientation, and fear among the general population. The focus of another reportage book, *Szachinszach*, published in English as *Shah of Shahs*,[7] is the violent overthrow of the Shah of Iran in 1979 and the beginning of the revolutionary period in the country's postwar history. Kapuściński paints a surprisingly cohesive picture of the tremendous changes in Iran via anecdotal stories, numerous eyewitness reports, massive amounts of notes and photographs, as he keeps searching for the meaning of the events in it all. The conclusion at which he arrives is that only several things remain stable throughout such drastic social changes: chaos, an overwhelming disconcertment, and – once the transformation is over – a certain sadness. *Heban*, known in the English-speaking world as *Shadow of the Sun*,[8] published in 1998, is yet another 'African' reportage in which Kapuściński employs a strategy similar to the one used in *Imperium* – a recapitulation of his several-decades-long encounter with the people and vast continent of Africa.

---

6   *Jeszcze dzień życia* – first Polish edition came out in 1976, published by Czytelnik in Warszawa, English translation came out as *Another day of life*, translated by William R. Brand, Katarzyna Mroczkowska-Brand, Klara Glowczewska, London: Penguin Books, 1988.

7   *Szachinszach*, Warszawa: Czytelnik, 1982, English translation by William R. Brand, Katarzyna Mroczkowska-Brand, San Diego: Harcourt Brace, Jovanovich, 1985.

8   First Polish edition by Czytelnik in Warszawa in 1998, English translation by Klara Glowczewska, New York: Vitage Books, 2001.

Typical journalistic devices, such as giving the exact dates of events, which he witnessed, the precise locations of places that he visited, or the political systems which control those places, are very scarce in *Shadow of the Sun*. As if in contradiction with this arguable imprecision, Kapuściński creates long, elaborate lists of simple, quotidian, often cheap objects and meticulously catalogues their use. This method of ascribing a strong presence to the objects generates a feeling of authenticity and the elusive verisimilitude of reportage. It should be clarified that I see Kapuściński's employment of objects similar to Heideggerian 'useful tools' and anchors in reality. The world reveals itself to us due to the 'usefulness' of objects, which serve as 'tools' for our contact with reality, as explained by Martin Heidegger in *Being and Time*. The objects also serve the author to describe the 'otherness' and to oppose the dominant Western discourse of mass ready-made consumerism; they are the vehicle of the stylistic innovations inherent in reportage.

The last four books Kapuściński authored, *Lapidarium VI* (2007), *Rwący nurt historii: Zapiski o XX i XXI wieku* (2007), *Dałem głos ubogim* (2008), and *O książkach, ludziach i sztuce* (2009), were published posthumously. Since 2009, only interviews with Kapuściński, accounts of his visits, and collections of his notes were published.

2. Style

Kapuściński's style – wry, subtle, and allusive – developed mostly in response to communist censorship, since many of his books – published prior to 1989 – were subjected to the scrutiny of the communist censors. Kapuściński was an extremely perceptive observer, and his keen and persuasive eyewitness accounts proved effective. Throughout his entire life, he relentlessly makes an effort to understand the processes and mechanisms regulating the apparent reality. Moreover, he has to experience everything himself, directly exposing himself to danger and suffering – often shocking contingencies and terrifying, albeit hilarious, events. The feelings, atmosphere, and intensity of a particular moment appropriated by his senses are crucial to his style. Kapuściński sympathizes with the Other and identifies with the people he invokes in his books, avoiding distance, mockery, and judgment. On the one hand, he does not capitalize on his boldness and courage, on the other, his efforts at presenting himself as a person equipped with essential fairness and integrity are a constant in his books. The effect is a distinctive style, which conveys the impression of being cool yet emphatic, self-effacing, and wise.

3. Typology of Kapuściński's reportage books

In *Lapidaria*, Kapuściński explains:

> I see myself as a researcher of Otherness – of other cultures, different ways of thinking, different behaviors. I want to encounter strangeness -- understood in its positive sense; strangeness which I like to come in contact with, in order to understand it. The question is always, how to describe present-day reality in a new and adequate way? Sometimes this kind of writing is called non-fiction writing. I would say that it's about non-fiction *creative* writing.[9]

The typology of Kapuściński's writing, or more precisely the issue of its belonging to the factual type of writing, is contested by many. His writing is often called 'anti-journalistic,' in the sense that for it, "the standard models of the journalistic reporting constitute the negative tradition of illusory objectivism and false neutrality."[10] Kapuściński creates his own kind of reportage, independent from the practices of mainstream, objectified journalism. Such typical journalistic devices as exact dates of events in which Kapuściński participates or precise locations of places he visits are scarce in many of his books. His method is to ask questions, collect notes, newspapers, and photographs, and reconstruct the story from memory at a later time. He rarely takes notes and often does not even use a recorder. His reportages are not pure-style journalism, but without exaggeration one can say they contain very effective storytelling, geo-political observation, and philosophical reflection, among other elements.

Correspondents are often accused of a voyeuristic fascination with observing human suffering [there is after all something morbidly entrancing or hideous in being everywhere in the world something atrocious or sensational happens]. Kapuściński's entire oeuvre, however, is an attempt to separate the corresponding and reporting of war from mainstream journalism. He writes to support his belief that correspondents do not just report but also have to function as the world's vicarious conscience. For Kapuściński, it is not just a job; bearing witness to suffering is a noble calling. Throughout his entire writing career, he presents himself as someone who indefatigably attempts to be humane and compassionate.

---

9 *Lapidaria*, p. 210 (translation and italics mine).
10 Ryszard Nycz, *Tekstowy świat: poststrukturalizm a wiedza o literaturze*, Warszawa: Instytut Badań Litearackich, 1995, p. 244 (translation my own).

4. Reporting: limiting and limitless

A reporter or correspondent is, among many other things, a translator of cultures. Thus, the reporter's subjectivity, as it exists between at least two cultures, is in a state of constant mediation and flux. The subjectivity has to be continuously negotiated between the two worlds in which he or she resides; in other words, the process of connecting two cultures is done by constructing a set of meanings that reflects both cultures simultaneously. In the field practice of reporting it is done (or should be done), among other techniques, through detailed observation and respectful participation, by focusing on the simple details of everyday existence. For many reporters it often means not endorsing the standard practices of journalism. In the preface to *Shadow of the Sun*, Kapuściński writes, "I avoided the official routes, palaces, important figures and big politics. I preferred to get a ride in a truck, wander with the nomads in the desert, be hosted by the peasants in the tropical savanna."[11] It has to be stated that he, of course, often did follow the main routes, visit capitols, imperial palaces, and headquarters of central powers. Yet, through simple stories of everyday existence, a reporter presents a picture of life in the far corners of the world and often gives voice to those who otherwise would never be heard. At the same time, a reporter has to submit to a limited version of the represented truth. He or she cannot physically be everywhere, talk to everyone, or take into account every possible fact while writing a story. The strength of reportage writings lies in its constant lack of faith in the one and only correct version of reality presented by this or that regime, ideology, or system. Reporters should consciously challenge conventions of the status quo, monolithic accounts of truth, and the ruling representatives of social authorities; and they can do it precisely by acknowledging an intentionally deficient picture of reality.

5. Launching of Kapuściński's career

Kapuściński's 'active participation approach' comes as no surprise when we consider his biography. With his childhood distorted, if not damaged, by the cruel events of World War II, he found himself during his formative years in the 'only true and right' system of post-war Communism in Poland. Similar to tens of thousands of his peers, with the naiveté and enthusiasm typical of young age, he claimed to have accepted the system as the only way to Poland's progress and growth, the only system that – in the eyes of Kapuściński's generation – was able to defeat the Nazis, bring freedom to Nazi-occupied Europe, and lead its

---

11 Ryszard Kapuściński, *Shadow of the Sun*, New York: Alfred A. Knopf, 2001, p. 204.

nations into a bright future. The author joined Związek Młodzieży Polskiej (Union of Polish Youth)[12] and embraced without any qualms its communist ideology while traveling across Poland and writing endless reports and numerous articles on 'improving the conditions of life of the working class.'[13] Or so he thought. In September 1955, he wrote an article entitled, "To też jest prawda o Nowej Hucie," (This too is the truth about Nowa Huta) for *Sztandar Młodych* in which he diligently exposed inhumane living conditions, ridiculously low salaries, prostitution, filth, hunger, violence, crime, and corruption among the workers of Nowa Huta.[14] A massive steelworks factory in the suburbs of Kraków, Nowa Huta was supposed to be the proof and paradigm of the efficiency and excellent organization of the Polish version of Communism; instead, it became a complete disaster. The article, commissioned by the higher Party functionaries as a response to Adam Ważyk's "Poemat dla dorosłych,"[15] a poem debunking communist myths and Stalinist propaganda, was supposed to undo the damage inflicted by the poem to the image of Nowa Huta and the system in general. Rather than doing that, the article became a definitive turning point in Kapuściński's life. The editor of *Sztandar Młodych* and several other individuals were fired, and Kapuściński had to hide among the workers of Nowa Huta. The upper management of the steelworks factory also lost their jobs, but some initiatives were undertaken, and the living conditions – as Kapuściński claimed later – improved for at least some workers in Nowa Huta.

The biggest paradox of his engaged article was yet to come. In the spring of 1956, there was a growing feeling that his earnest and straightforward engagement was becoming too uncomfortable for the system, which itself was about to be shaken dramatically for the first time after World War II by the strikes in Poznań in October of 1956. As a result of some upper–level Party machinations, quite surprisingly, Kapuściński's career as a reporter was about to be launched; he was sent as a foreign correspondent on his very first assignment abroad, pretty much as far from Poland as then possible. He was sent to India. This trip did not, of course, happen without reason. On January 26, 1950, India became a republic with Jawaharlal Nehru as Prime Minister. The country became part of the

---

12 Związek Młodzieży Polskiej (Union or Association of Polish Youth, abbr. ZMP) was a Polish communist youth organization, existing from 1948 to 1956. It was subordinated to Polish Workers' Party and acted as a tool of political indoctrination towards the youth. Source: http://en.wikipedia.org/wiki/ Związek_Młodzieży_Polskiej

13 Beata Nowacka, Zygmunt Ziątek, *Ryszard Kapuściński: Biografia pisarza*, Kraków: Wydawnictwo Znak, 2008, p. 50.

14 Ryszard Kapuściński, „To też jest prawda o Nowej Hucie" ("This too is the truth about Nowa Huta"), *Sztandar Młodych*, (Sep 30, 1955) No. 234.

15 Adam Ważyk, "Poemat dla dorosłych," *Nowa Kultura*, (Aug 1955), No. 34.

Non-Aligned Movement while cooperating with the Soviet Union and the countries of the Communist Bloc. Because of this cooperation, the Soviet Union agreed to sell airplanes and weapons to India, and Prime Minister Nehru visited Poland.[16] Kapuściński's trip was a direct consequence of the political situation and the Soviet Union's interests in India.

I am far from claiming that with publishing "To też jest prawda o Nowej Hucie," Kapuściński abandoned his idealistic and naïve activist beliefs. For many years to come, his writing bore a clear mark of his Marxist upbringing. I would venture to say that Kapuściński's impromptu journey to the Congo in 1961 during the so-called Congo Crisis, where for the first time he witnessed a coup (the murder of Patrice Lumumba in Stanleyville), incredible chaos, violence, and life-threatening situations – instead of happy Congoans taking their country from the hands of Belgian colonizers – seriously weakened the author's naïve faith in the vindictive fairness of the dialectics that was supposed to be present in historical processes. I think that only at the beginning of the 1970s Kapuściński, and only to a certain extent, liberated himself from the narrow brackets of his youthful mindset and the restraints of speaking on behalf of an ideological necessity, of a larger-than-life systemic project, of historical justice, etc. The result of this sometimes difficult freedom is an analysis of totalitarian power remarkably deprived of his previous juvenile exaltation and naïve engagement entitled *The Emperor: Downfall of an Autocrat*.

---

16   Source: http://pl.wikipedia.org/wiki/Jawaharlal_Nehru

II. Reportage – Historical Overview and Theory

Often described as a hybrid genre, or as a peripheral type of writing, reportage is also referred to as 'long form journalistic narrative,' 'documentary novel,' or as a form of 'social document.' Reportage essentially encompasses texts, which take as their subject matter actually-existing people, societies, and cultures and adopt various components of both journalistic and fictional texts. Such texts base their stories on empirically validated truth and they claim to reproduce reality in a seemingly unmediated way. It also stands to reckon that while reportage books have value for empirical sciences, they mostly are appreciated for the elucidation of the reading public.

The main feature of the master narrative of the Polish reportage which I analyze in this study entails the encounter of a radical Other met during travels to distant lands. The reportage writer then digests and reflects on the travel experience and mediates/translates his or her encounter for the reader, who is unlikely to have such an experience. The crucial element of the narrative is a direct engagement with a somehow disadvantaged or underprivileged community, as in the case of the war-ridden African countries stricken with starvation and/or tyrannical power, or the confused and scared residents of extremely chaotic post-Soviet Russia. In this type of writing then, the ethical aspect and the epistemological responsibility of the author toward the represented communities and the author's moral duty in telling their stories in a conscientious manner should remain the central focus. In this book, I analyze whether this guiding principle has any influence on the manner in which reportage participates in discussing the role of media and literature in today's society.

6. Short history

It can be stated that before the collapse of communism, reportage in Poland was traditionally suspicious of the dominant communist ideology that more or less successfully attempted to impose its rules over reality. Later, after 1989, in a growing disappointment towards the reality of the newly-introduced capitalism, reportage continued to question the dominant discourse of the new reality while attempting to represent and interpret the world in a fashion that many believed to be credible and responsible. Reportage traditionally held itself at a distance from mainstream (sometimes also called "objective" – the quotation marks are important here) journalism, since typical journalistic texts were supposed to be comprehensive and often attempted to achieve critical closure.

In the second half of the twentieth century in Poland (before 1989), the main, ostensibly "objective" stream of journalism was in the employ of the ruling Communist Party, and it presented a distorted reality in such a way as to serve the totalitarian system. At the same time, reportage often tried to oppose that system by depicting Third World societies and cultures; through these descriptions and characteristically Aesopian language reportage deceived censors and smuggled illegitimate information, which was unerringly deciphered by Polish readership. Reportage, by using direct descriptions of reality, which often only pretended at objectivity, was ironically quite effective at condemning that world in an environment of omnipresent censorship. Kapuściński's writing, precisely because it was presented as non-fiction and emulated journalistic objectivity, allowed people living under communist censorship to reflect upon questions of totalitarian power and individual responsibility.

In the twentieth century, reportage has moved from newspaper columns into book-length writings. Disagreements continue among literary scholars as to what exactly has caused such a growth of interest in this genre that straddles the border between literature and journalism. The experience of twentieth century totalitarianisms and readers' distrust of fictive works are believed to bear significant impact on the development of non-fiction writing, along with other factors such as the educational revolution, the supposed self-destruction of the novel, and new generations of authors who intended to manifest the truth (whatever the truth was believed by them to be). There is a consensus that in Poland the history of this type of writing started to play a significant role in the literary scene before World War II – during the interwar period, or *Dwudziestolecie*.[17] During that period, Melchior Wańkowicz, an important figure in Polish reportage, created his own tradition of literary journalism, which he understood as his own style of storytelling.[18] In it, he combined the authenticity of facts with elements of memoir and anecdote-like vignettes; its language was terse, vivid, and fresh. In the form he used – half epic, half lyric, often shifting from irony to pathos – Wańkowicz stylistically appealed to the tradition of the Baroque *gawęda szlachecka* (gentry-like storytelling). His works, written prior to World War II, created abroad after his flight to Romania in September 1939, as well as those composed after the author's return to Poland in 1958, are simultaneously innovative and seminal to the creation of this particular tradition of Polish reportage. However,

---

17   Zygmunt Ziątek. *Wiek dokumentu: Inspiracje dokumentarne w polskiej prozie współczesnej*. Warszawa: IBL, 1999.
18   See for example: Ziółkowska, *Blisko Wańkowicza*, Kraków : Wydawnictwo Literackie, 1975; Kazimierz Wolny, *Sztuka reportażu wojennego Melchiora Wańkowicza*, Rzeszów: Wydawnictwo Wyższej Szkoły Pedagogicznej w Rzeszowie, 1991; Mieczysław Kurzyna; *Wańkowicz*, Warszawa: Authors Agency, 1972.

the tradition of reportage, with its focus on direct contact with a disadvantaged community affording few evaluative statements and authorial comments, was initiated in Poland by Zofia Nałkowska. Many of her works combine features of fiction and non-fiction, with the author often becoming one of the characters. At the same time, she closely follows the historical and social transformations of the nation from which she draws material for broad generalizations concerning the individual and collective consciousness. Elements of reportage can already be seen in her collection of prison stories *Ściany świata* (*Walls of the World*),[19] written in 1931, where she reflects on the untraceable origins of evil, the social conditioning of its understanding, and crimes often unjustly punished. In *Medallions*,[20] once again, Nałkowska rarely uses normative declarations or remarks; only the facts function as testimony as they are astonishing in their immediacy to the Nazi crimes. The book is entirely based on shocking facts, which the author heard and witnessed immediately after World War II during her work for the Nazi Crimes Investigating Commission.

Nałkowska's method, possibly as a sign of the post-war readership's faith in the pre-war writing's authenticity – that is, an unquestionably reliable testimony of direct contact with a community living in an exceptional situation and with the focus on contemporaneity and actuality of facts – continued to play an important role during the communist period and in newly independent Poland.

In Poland, where the communist system was imposed by force and then supported by the constant presence of the Soviet troops, as well as the immediate, always threatening proximity of the Soviet Union, the nation's living conditions were far from First World standards. The absurdity, grotesqueness, and abnormality that pervaded life in the PRL (Polska Rzeczpospolita Ludowa – Polish People's Republic) created a milieu conducive to a significant growth of reportage. Jane Leftwich Curry, in her book *Poland's Journalists: Professionalism and Politics*, explains how various types of journalistic writing were

> vehicles for veiled discussions of theoretical or political issues in which the author does not have to explicitly state the problem, his position, or recommendations ... In interviews [conducted by Curry], journalists also saw [these styles] as the most useful vehicles for bypassing censorship and affecting social policy. With these methods, press criticism often is artfully argued so that Party stands and statements integrate with criticism of these very stands. With these methods, subjects prohibited by censors are presented indirectly through more literary writing. [The author] becomes more skillful, tries to trick the censor, winks at the reader, uses dodges, allusions, plays on words.[21]

---

19 Zofia Nałkowska, *Ściany świata*, Warszawa: Gebethner i Wolf, 1931.
20 Nałkowska, *Medaliony*, Warszawa: Czytelnik, 1946; *Medallions*, English translation by Diana Kuprel, Evanston, IL: Northwestern University Press, 2000.
21 Curry, ed. Cambridge: Cambridge University Press, 1990, p. 192.

The political system contributed to the growth of reportage as the very other or opposition *against* which reportage writing drew its popularity. The circumstances in which reportage was developing were at the same time not very favorable to traditional journalistic writing; that is, writing in an open and directly persuasive style, expressing judgments and opinions, and striving to present objective facts. Coding the truth so it could survive censorship by using Aesopian language during the communist period, and the technique of placing importance on carefully selected, apparently peripheral topics are central to understanding the phenomenon of Polish post-war reportage.

7. Theory
a. truth claim

> "What is truth?"
>
> Pontius Pilate (John, 18:38)

John C. Hartsock, a scholar of reportage, introduces an appealing view of the genre. He claims that reportage text "reads like a novel or a short story except that it is true or makes a truth claim to reflecting phenomenal experience."[22] In contrast to fiction, reportage has a clearly recognizable phenomenological foundation. At the same time, reportage texts contain many characteristics which most fictional texts exhibit as well, such as character development, third-person narration, development of plot, and most importantly suspension of judgment. Reportage relies on its extratextual referents (reality, the world), while judgment of fiction's referents' verifiability is suspended (irrelevant). The world to which fiction refers is recognized as a creation that is neither true nor false, or at least the distinction between the truth and falsity is negligible.

Hartsock uses the following description for it:

> The critic might ... examine the form [reportage—K.K.] according to its epistemological fluidity, a fluidity that nonetheless can establish an approximate critical site for investigation. That site is composed of the "facts" that there is no name for the form; that other forms, discourses, and genres can fit into it or dominate it or overlap it; that the limitations of a selecting subjectivity in the form ensure the lack of critical omniscience; and that phenomena are ultimately fluid given that how we see the world determines what we see. Like the chameleon, the form changes color according to the mode of questioning brought to bear on it. By acknowledging this, we gain greater insight into the nature of such literary "factions" as part of a larger

---

22 John C. Hartsock, "'Literary Journalism' as an Epistemological Moving Object Within a Larger 'Quantum' Narrative," *Journal of Communication Inquiry* 23:4 (October 1999).

"quantum narrative" of interpretation or approximation, not a narrative of neatly delineated certainty (432).

The authenticity of the facts presented in reportage has to be unquestionable; however, its practitioners make sure to reserve their right to choose the context and to model the whole composition according to the criteria, which they select. The reader assumes that the people's lives presented in this type of writing really transpired. Moreover, the appeal of what actually happened has a particular ability to move the reader in a way that fiction does not, or at least in a way differing from fiction. Fictive literary works have a history of critical readings and interpretation; even if they attempt to represent the world, the truth or falsity of such representation is irrelevant. Such an approach forces the reader to have an aesthetic (not evaluative) judgment of those works and removes them from a political or historical context. "The result of this aestheticizing process is to render literary narrative something we regard as neither true nor false; [however] nonfiction is thought of as the realm of discourse where true and false are important distinctions."[23]

Fiction is the 'document of an époque' (its consciousness, rituals, customs, etc.), presenting that which is typical, common, repeatable, or legitimized by myth or literariness; nonfiction narratives pay attention to facts and shorten the aesthetic distance between fact and fiction.[24] A documentary form of narrative which should be based on an immediate proximity to facts becomes a part of a collectively created world, and the collectivity factor is presumed to protect it against entering the realm of ideology.[25] Facts freed from being utilized as mere temporary arguments reach "a naïve and solemn meaning," akin to the type of meaning which Czesław Miłosz ascribes to reality.[26] Roman Ingarden's analysis of truth in literature is even more helpful. He compares various versions of truth and concludes that truth in literature is different than in logic and real life. He

---

23 Phyllis Frus, *The Politics and Poetics of Journalistic Narrative: The Timely and the Timeless*, Cambridge: Cambridge University Press, 1994, p. 74.
24 Jerzy Jarzębski, "Między 'realizmem' a 'prawdą': proza krajowa po wojnie," *W Polsce czyli wszędzie*, Kraków: Zielona Sowa, 2000. It should be stated though that in the article Jarzębski talks about "documentary type of writing," not about "reportaż" *per se*.
25 *Ibid.* p. 117. Jarzębski also maintains that another good example of such situations are works of Miron Białoszewski – although most of them poetic, some were close to reportage. Białoszewski's works are, in Jarzębski's opinion, fascinating examples of an utterly moral approach to presenting facts. Through them (facts), Białoszewski proposes a general healing of people, and not of some kind of abstract truth, hence comes his proposition of existence in an immediate approximation to facts.
26 Czesław Miłosz, "Nobel Lecture – Odczyt w Akademii Szwedzkiej," New York: Farrar Straus Giroux, 1981, p. 191.

forges his idea of "quasi assertive sentences" as the peculiar form of conveying truth in literature, which pertains equally to fiction and nonfiction.[27]

A writer embraces the world in a creative gesture, imposing his or her own truth or sense on reality, and so every description of reality is conveyed through someone's particular perspective. One can attempt to represent the world in literature (if at all) only if one has sufficient tools; these tools have to allow the artist to reasonably oscillate between his own phenomenal experience and a holistic concept of reality. In presenting his or her concept of reality, an author has to be well aware of the danger of a single 'right' concept of reality which every ideology tries to force on the world. A singular universal and unchanging perspective of reality does not exist. However, in communism, 'objective and scientific laws of historical progress' decided which of the observed facts were deemed to be true. A writer trying to describe facts was obliged to see the world as represented in the communist system's handbooks. The world had clear divisions, the criteria were unambiguous and the author's personal experience was supposed to help eliminate the elements that did not fit the universal mode of totalitarianism. That was the power of assumption, and this *a priori* knowledge attempted to achieve complete supremacy over phenomenal experience; moreover, it aspired to hegemonic reality.

In literature and art, the concept of 'truth' has a wide range of significance and provokes many questions and doubts. In fictive literature, judgment of truth and falsehood is suspended (however, not always, as literature can be mimetic and employ common sense) and therefore it is aesthetic. If there is no ideology (for example communism) sorting out the doubts about truth and falsity, the attempt to understanding what the truth actually is becomes almost unfathomable. Truth in a literary work is relative, it undergoes historical changes, it transforms according to modifications in poetics and social situations. What is true in one period of time can be viewed as a convention in another, and while the truth is a product of culture in a different period, it definitely is not absolute but constantly evolving. The representation of truth then constitutes one of the cognitive elements of a literary genre. Literary truth should not be identified with any concrete historical styles or poetics since the *raison d'etre* of such poetics is that it offers readers what they are convinced to see as true.[28]

---

27 Roman Ingarden, "On So-called 'Truth' in Literature," Jean G. Harrell and Alina Wierzbiańska, ed., *Aesthetics in Twentieth-century Poland: Selected Essays*, translated by Adam Czerniawski, Lewisburg, Pa., Bucknell University Press, 1973.
28 Michał Głowiński, *Gry powieściowe. Szkice z teorii i historii form naracyjnych*, Warszawa: Państwowe Wydawnictwa Naukowe, 1973.

Truth is an element of a literary work, but at the same time, it constitutes a crucial element of the relation between the literary work and the reader's consciousness. Therefore, a literary work not only constantly refers to extratextual reality but also forces the reader to sort out and form his or her knowledge about that reality. Getting involved in the process of reading means accepting a certain convention, and such involvement (in the process of reading) equals sacrificing the criteria of cognition used for everyday reality. Truth in a literary work stands in relation to other statements in that work and not to real world accounts. However, it should be noted that the truth in a literary work is only one of the elements of literature understood as a convention; literature's cognitive ability cannot and should not be reduced to that of recording the truth.

b. coherence vs. correspondence

Modern theories of fictional representation follow a clear division between factuality and fictionality. For instance, New Critical theories state that fiction is highly ordered, but that it has little to do with reference. William Wimsatt and Cleanth Brooks state that fictive forms direct their objective toward coherence ('narrative' – addition mine), while factual forms – at correspondence ('communication of the facts' – addition mine).[29] Northrop Frye follows their example when he says that "the final direction of meaning" in fiction is inward (based on intratextual referents), while in nonfiction, which he calls "descriptive or assertive writing," the direction is outward (extratextual referents).[30] Another way of understanding reportage is seeing it as a space where an old philosophical dilemma, which is the tension between truth (facts, information) and beauty (fiction, literariness), is unfolding. Examining this dialectic can help in forming a taxonomy of this writing form more precisely, since reportage can either approach its informative value and become more of a news cast, or move toward its literary aspect, and develop into a fictional narrative. "The greater the coherence or internal direction of the text, the lesser its obligation to make verifiable statements about historical world. Beauty and Truth exist in inverse proportion to one another."[31] The more a text is directed externally the higher its obligation to stay true to its extratex-

---

29 William K. Wimsatt & Cleanth Brooks, *Literary Criticism: A Short History*, New York: Knopf, 1957.
30 Northrop Frye, *The Anatomy of Criticism: Four Essays*, Princeton: Princeton University Press, 1957.
31 Barbara Foley, *Telling the Truth: The Theory and Practice of Documentary Fiction*, Ithaca and London: Cornell University Press, 1986, p. 75.

tual referents. In other words, correspondence in a nonfiction text has a higher ethical value than its aesthetical coherence.

c. truth vs. volatilization

Characterizing reportage can be done by placing it in opposition to mainstream journalism. In his 1873 essay "Truth and Falsity in Their Ultramoral Sense," Friedrich Nietzsche describes a predisposition for totalizing distinctive phenomenal experiences into wide-ranging abstract simplification and about erasing the differences between those experiences.[32] According to him, such cognitive process is mediated by language. The abstracting character of mainstream journalism (which tries to be comprehensive, depends on a formula, provides summary of the news, attempts to achieve critical closure, etc.) can be seen as a result of cognitive totalizing. Reportage, however, places itself on the opposite side of this dialectic since it focuses on the phenomenal experience of an independent subject (a reporter). The main feature of the phenomenal is that it is distinctive, unique, individual; therefore, the phenomenal is capable of resisting critical totalization. Reportage attempts to stand in opposition with dominant discourse of mainstream journalism because it is, among other things, often non- or anti-journalistic, indefinable and anti-totalizing.[33]

It can also be said, following Walter Benjamin, that mainstream objectified journalism creates a cognitive gap between the phenomenal world of individual experience and a far-off world that contains information about that experience. Mainstream or objectified journalism often has a depersonalizing nature. Readers are alienated from the facts they are reading by the epistemological nature of objectified journalism. Reportage tries to narrow that gap between the individual experience and the physical world by engaging, among other things, the subjectivity of the reporter. Therefore, such subjective story-telling, contrary to the mainstream journalism, is never omniscient. It also emphasizes its subjective and collective aspects, which protect it from being usurped by ideology. Mainstream journalism, precisely because of its aspiring to objectivity, can and often does become compromised by being in the service of the dominant social discourse.

---

32 Friedrich Nietzsche, "On Truth and Falsity in Their Ultramoral Sense," translated by M. Mugge, Vol. 48 of *Philosophical Writings*, ed. E. Grimm and C. Molina y Media, New York: Continuum, 1995, p. 97.
33 Nycz, *Tekstowy...*, p. 244.

d. authority in reportage texts

Since representation is always limitation, as Jean Francois Lyotard says, attention should be given to the way the truth is presented as well as the manner in which a text asserts its authority over what it claims to be true.[34] The distinctive feature of factual writing is the presence of empirically provable statements that have, or at least should have, the authority of truth. Hence, non-fiction becomes a realm where the author has an enormous power over truth, or whatever he or she decides to present as truth. Thomas Couser's explanation of the question of authority in non-fiction writing is useful in examining this problem: it is "the authority of its grounding in a verifiable relationship between the text and an extratextual referent."[35]

Authority should not be simply understood as verifiability, as we tend to verify mainly the truth/lie dichotomy; authority is the agent which sanctions the opposition. Even if we know that simple association of textual statements to verifiable extratextual facts is of narrow practical use, we still have to take into consideration the method of choosing those facts. Non-fiction writing always has an element of selection, since it is impossible to describe everything or to cover all the facts in a story. For that reason, even the most meticulously documented narrative will always be somehow imperfect, "and partiality (in the sense of incompletion) begets partiality (in the sense of bias)."[36]

Gerard Genette, in the article "Vraisemblance et motivation," challenges the traditional understanding of the causal order in a narrative discourse, which states that discursive means determine narrative ends.[37] Genette's view on it is the opposite: a narrator forms the beginning and middle of a narration as a result of the predetermined ends. Thus, narratives are constructed in an order that is reverse to the traditional understanding of them: the outcome determining that which precedes it. The final textual product is an effect of "les determinations retrogrades . . . des moyens par les fins, et, pour parler plus brutalement, des causes par les effets" (94). Genette also clarifies the notion of *la vraisemblance*; he says that the narrative content pretends to be the "motivation" for the linear unfolding of narrative discourse where cause should determine effect. However, Gennette suggests that narrative discourse, which is largely characterized by a fundamental arbitrariness, can be also called "motivation." And it is there, in the "motivation" in which the arbitrary elements of a story are hidden, that they lie

---

34   Jean Francois Lyotard, *The Postmodern Condition: A Report on Knowledge*, Minneapolis: University of Minnesota Press, 1984.
35   G. Thomas Couser, *Altered Egos*, New York: Oxford University Press, 1989.
36   *Ibid.* p. 122.
37   Gerard Genette, "Vraisemblance et motivation," *Communications* 11 (1968).

beneath "un masque de determination causale" (96). In other words, Genette says that motivation is an "alibi causaliste" (97), which gives narratives an arbitrary teleological order. Consequently, this layer of each narrative, the "motivation," constitutes the part of every reportage text where the process of selecting facts occurs and where the authority over truth is most evident.

Establishing authority over truth in a literary work is by no means a concept easy to define. In some cases, for instance in traditional cultures, authority can be viewed as communal: if the details of a story are not factual, the stories are culturally authentic.[38] Such cultures do not see an individual as a separate entity, they also do not recognize an author as an originator; their stories, even autobiographies, are collaborative, not individual efforts.

In the words of Mikhail Bakhtin:

> The word in language is half someone else's. It becomes one's own only when the speaker populates it with his own intention, his own accent, when he appropriates the word, adapting it to his own semantic and expressive intention. Prior to this moment of appropriation, the word does not exist in a neutral and impersonal language (it is not, after all, out of a dictionary that a speaker gets his words!), but rather it exists in other people's mouths, in other people's contexts, serving other people's intentions: it is from there that one must take the word, and make it one's own.[39]

Authority is not solely established by a verifiability of extratextual facts, nor does it originate in the primordial nature of language; it must constantly be negotiated and renegotiated. "[O]ne premise of a dialogical approach to life-writing might be that the authority of an autobiography is proportional to the narrator's recognition and articulation of threats to it."[40]

e. encountering the other

The Other described in reportage books analyzed in this study is one foreign and unfamiliar to the Polish reader; he or she most often is from Africa or the Middle East. It can also be one of Poland's feared "others" – the vast spaces of the European and Asian parts of Russia, described in *Imperium*. Kapuściński, often simultaneously employed as a war and/or press correspondent for Polish newspapers or news agencies, undertook long and perilous journeys in order to gain a thorough knowledge of the people's lives he described. While abroad, the author experienced the hardship of traveling to underdeveloped countries, including

---

38 Maxine Hong Kinston, *The Woman Warrior*, New York: Vintage, 1977.
39 Mikhail Bakhtin, *The Dialogic Imagination*, trans. Caryl Emerson and Michael Holquist, Austin: University of Texas Press, 1981.
40 Couser, *Altered egos...*, p. 134.

endangering his life. As a result of the author's intense involvement and active participation, his narratives attain high credibility in the eyes of the reader.

Detailed relations, reflections, and descriptions of the author's personal experiences, encountering other cultures and "the otherness," constitute a crucial element of reportage narratives. According to Jacques Lacan, it is through the existence of the Other that we can create, if only for a moment, a wholeness in our fragmented subjectivity. We depend on the Other, both to create the self through difference and to fill the gap created by our subjectivity, since communion with the Other represents the ideal self we have lost. In such communion lies the truth, says Lacan.[41] Such a view of the Other facilitates an approach in which the disadvantaged community is the central focus of a reportage text. On the other hand, Lacan's understanding of the "radical Other" is such that the Other is one with whom we have nothing in common, an other who is completely different and distant from us. This radicality of the Other, however, ought not to prevent the knowing subject (in this case, a reportage writer) from undertaking every effort to learn about the Other. Such epistemological responsibility of an author is best explained by Emmanuel Levinas' view of the Other. Levinas sees the Other as one with a face, to which we have to turn and for which we have to take full responsibility. In order to attempt understanding and being fully responsible for the Other, we have to enter the Other's world, engage it, get to know "the dramatic event of being-in-the-world."

Levinas says explicitly:

> We are responsible beyond our intentions. ... Our relation with the other certainly consists in wanting to understand him, but this relation exceeds the confines of understanding. Not only because, besides curiosity, knowledge of the other also demands sympathy or love, ways of being that are different from impassive contemplation, but also because, in our relation to the other, the latter does not affect us by means of a concept. The other is a being and counts as such.[42]

f. reality and fictionality

While researching, I have come to the conclusion that many contemporary theorists of nonfiction seem to be concerned with "the unreality of reality and the undecidability of discourse."[43] In other words, critics and theorists of nonfiction are

---

41 Jacques Lacan, "Introduction of the Big Other," *The Seminar of Jacques Lacan*, Book II, ed. Jacques-Alain Miller, translated by Sylvana Tomaselli, New York: W. W. Norton, 1988, p. 244.
42 Emmanuel Levinas, *On Thinking of the Other. Entre Nous*, trans. by Michael B. Smith and Barbara Hershav, New York: Columbia University Pres, 1991, p. 4.
43 Foley, *Telling...*, p. 11.

troubled with the disappearing border (distinction) between fiction and nonfiction, the blurring of erstwhile clear lines between reality and fiction, and the impossibility of defining the distinctive features of both types of writing. Mas'ud Zavarzadeh, for example, describes the poetics of the nonfiction novel thus: "[It] is a narrative which is simultaneously self-referential and out-referential, factual and fictional, and thus well equipped to deal with the elusive effusion of fact and fiction which has become the matrix of today's experience."[44] Zavarzadeh claims that the "factuality" of current experience breaks away from monoreferential narratives, which necessitate an unambiguous pledge either to fact or fiction. Many agree with Jacques Derrida, who states that the very formulation of genre distinctions is undermined by the subversive nature of writing. Robert Scholes goes even further when he states: "All writing, all composition is construction. We do not imitate the world, we construct versions of it. There is no mimesis, only poesis. No recording, only constructing."[45] Theorists seem ready to affirm that factual and fictive discourses are not unchangeable monoliths but types of writing that transform alongside societies and times.[46] Although the increasing difficulty of distinguishing between fiction and nonfiction seems still to be causing a certain anxiety among literary theorists, the turn of the millennium has brought about a visible shift toward ethics in the theories of representation, or more precisely, toward the ethical aspect linked to representing lives of actually-existing people. The ethical aspect of representing reality understood as thoroughly getting to know lives of other people, societies, and cultures and later describing and demonstrating them in the form of books, as demonstrated by Ryszard Kapuściński, is what I address in the chapters of the book.

One of the major claims of my book is that the master narrative of encountering "otherness" present in reportage books encourages a cautious and careful approach to the facts being described. I see the master narrative as a constant negotiation between the authorial vantage and the extratextual world, between the dry reality of facts and the creative act of writing, over which the ethical aspect should constantly be in control.

---

44 Mas'ud Zavarzadeh, *The Mythopoeic Reality: The Postwar American Nonfiction Novel*, Urbana: University of Illinois Press, 1976, p. 57.
45 Robert Scholes, *Structural Fabulation: An Essay on the Fiction of the Future*, Notre Dame: University of Notre Dame Press, 1975, p. 7.
46 It also should be noted that Polish theorists made a significant contribution to theories of mimesis and representation (see Michał Głowiński, Ryszard Nycz, Zygmunt Ziątek, Anna Łebkowska, et al.) Yet little, to date, has been written in Poland on the ethical aspect of reportage writing.

III. Constant Negotiation

"The sun of truth strikes each part of the earth at a little different angle."[47] In a 1906 *Scribner's* article, an unidentified author writes, "[Non-fiction is an] endeavor to reproduce, sometimes dramatically, sometimes incidentally, the incompleteness of life. Then, too, the newspaper usually depicts life as it is embodied in a constantly shifting series of individuals, selected haphazardly."[48] Reportage tries to reveal phenomenal experience based on the reporter's experiences and his or her manner of examining those experiences. The technique a reportage writer uses to ask questions about his or her phenomenal experience is central to the method of determining his or her knowledge about it, since, as we learn through the Heisenberg principle, our knowledge of the world is determined by the kind of questions we pose.[49]

According to Immanuel Kant, "knowledge [is] the product of a *creative synthesis of the imagination*," and it situates the subject at the center of the epistemological process.[50] Hence, the subject has to be constantly conscious of his or her central place and agency in the cognitive practice. "A person can be judged responsible or irresponsible only as she/he is clearly regarded as an agent (in this case a cognitive agent) in the circumstances in question."[51] A reporter, who due to the nature of his or her profession, constantly engages in the knowledge-seeking process, has to be fully aware of his/her epistemic responsibility and the consequences of his/her actions that affect both the culture being studied and his/her own. A reporter during his or her travels to foreign countries becomes a field anthropologist, submerging him- or herself in a new cultural experience. An extremely important matter is that in such situations, harm can be easily inflicted upon that other culture while experiencing it (the field of anthropological ethics comes to the rescue here). Reportage often operates in areas or communities rendered marginal by various conditions. The unquestioned priority of such nonfiction writing should then be the effect on such community or individuals belonging (or assigned) to it. "Deliberation of the ethics of life writing entails

---

47 Garland Hamlin, [1894] reprint from 1960, *Crumbling Idols*, Cambridge, MA: Harvard University Press.
48 "Point of View: The Newspaper and Fiction," *Scribner's Magazine* 40 (1906): 122-24.
49 W. Heisenberg, *Physics and Philosophy: The Revolution in Modern Science,* New York: Harper and Row, 1958.
50 Lorraine Code, *Epistemic Responsibility*, Hanover, NH: Brown University Press, 1987, p. 99 (italics added by L. Code)
51 *Ibid.* p. 51.

weighing competing values: the desire to tell one's story and the need to protect others, the obligation to truth and the obligations of trust."[52]

Through the process of translating the studied culture into the language of our own culture, the perception of the reporter's original culture changes dramatically and allows for a better comprehension of it. Every time a reporter attempts to learn about a new culture, he or she experiments with and changes his or her own culture. The text of a reportage piece exposes the reader to an alienating sense of otherness and encourages the reader to try to overcome it. In order to do so, the reader is obliged to try to integrate herself with the Other. The texts by themselves are incomplete; they become complete only by being read. However, reportage texts not only make the reader ponder universal truths, but they become a call to action precisely because of their authenticity and factual basis. Reading them enables a sense of otherness that has a potential for change, to make the reader examine and alter his or her own system of values.

The epistemic responsibility of a reporter, in spite of him or her being painfully aware that reality (community, environment, as well as nature of the knower, among other things) is a constraining factor in the cognitive process, requires ensuring that the cultures represented in reportage books possess the fundamental right to be as innovative and as productive as the reporter's own culture.

In my book I try to demonstrate the complex ethical problems a reportage text inevitably entails. I claim that there are countless factors participating in the process of creating nonfiction, and they are often beyond the control of both the author and the people being portrayed. In my opinion, such factors as language, politics, history, traditions, customs undeniably have to be confronted in reportage texts. However, these texts are in a sense already controlled by all those issues, so they definitely do not need any more restricting, either by the author (such as overprotecting the subjects) or the reader.

No subjectivity can function without discourse; however, that does not imply subjectivity is a passive product of language: "Style is not simply an effusion of self, nor is it mere adherence to prevailing norms of usage and decorum. Rather it is to be found in the *tension* between the two, between the writer and his community of discourse, idiolect and dialect."[53] It should also be recapitulated that nonfiction writing is a constant negotiation – a negotiation between the horrible and the disguised as honorable but in fact questionable need to bear witness.

---

52 G. Thomas Couser, *Vulnerable Subjects: Ethics and Life Writing*, Ithaca and London: Cornell University Press, 2004.
53 Joseph Harris, "The Plural Text/The Plural Self: Roland Barthes and William Cole," *College English*, No. 2 (February 1987): 158:170. Italics mine.

Kapuściński more or less humorously deems the type of writing he employs an empty field which he is "trying to cultivate" (*Lapidaria I*, 204). The process of "cultivating" reportage is strongly shaped by the elements of theories presented above. In the parts of my book following this Introduction, I am analyzing the effect and presence of the elements of reportage theories, concentrating mainly on the ethical aspect of non-fiction writing and on the tyranny of the narratorial grip, which I perceive as one of the crucial forces dictating the form, content, and authenticity of a reportage work.

Part Two
TYRANNY

I. The Useful Discord

The Emperor: The Downfall of an Autocrat (*Cesarz*) was published for the first time in Poland by Czytelnik in 1978. It was translated into English by William R. Brand and Katarzyna Mroczkowska-Brand, and published by Harcourt Brace Jovanovich in 1982.[54] The main narrative of the book describes the last years before the 1974 collapse of Haile Selassie's more than 40-year long tyranny in Ethiopia. It also tells a story of two worlds in conflict expressed with the use of two idioms representing the opposite worlds, both struggling with their appropriate ideologies. The conflict is masterfully expressed through the dynamic interplay of the two idioms: that of the emperor's courtiers living in enormous luxury and that of the narrator who places himself as a representative of the rest of society, which is fighting extreme poverty and starvation.

The structure of the book is precise and symmetrical: there are three chapters: "Tron" (Throne), "Idzie, idzie" (It's Coming, It's Coming), and "Rozpad" (The Collapse). Each chapter is approximately fifty pages long and each one is introduced by two pages of seemingly random quotations. The layout of the book adds to the feeling of encountering a meticulously planned structure: each courtier tells his own story, which begins with his initials given at the beginning of the story ('his,' since no women speak in the book, this is a 'man's world'). The courtiers tell their stories in a manner of a recorded interview – addressing the narrator directly, often using verbs in the second person singular form. Their narratives are printed in a regular font. The narrator's words, which are inserted between the courtiers' stories, are always italicized. The structure of the book is symmetrical, precise, almost severe. The narrator's narratives break apart the court's discourse and constitute the counterbalance for it. All the elements of the book's discourse complete each other and create one entity. Even though at first glance, the narrator's insertions and the courtiers' stories might seem to stand in a discord, *The Emperor* cannot exist without both of the elements.

> His [Kapuściński's] method of telling the story is deceptively simple: he allows people to speak, and the result is a collage of often unattributed voices. It is a kind of verbal post-mortem. He makes no pretence that his is legitimate 'straight' journalism built from 'attributable sources,' and he has admitted many times that his practices would be unacceptable to *The New York Times* and most other serious newspapers.[55]

Kapuściński, famously enough, very rarely recorded conversations with his interlocutors – he felt that recording their words made them uncomfortable and

---

54   All quotations *The Emperor* are from these two editions.
55   Carl Tighe, "Ryszard Kapuściński and *The Emperor*," *The Modern Language Review* 91: 4 (Oct 1996): 927.

caused their self-censorship. He also rarely took notes during interviews. His notes were sparse, random. Consequently, let us not forget that the courtiers' 'statements' and 'testimonies' are in fact Kapuściński's memories and impressions written a long time after he had actually met with Selassie's courtiers. People in the book are *characters, created* by the author, and they tell stories *not* of actually existing persons, but of compilations of people. It should be restated that the discourse of the book is a creation that is only loosely based on reality. This is not strict fact-gripping reporting from the world's latest hotspot. The facts are made to serve a purpose, they are carefully chosen and cut to shape – such situation opens up the space for the narrator's tight rule of the book's discourse.

1. Tension between two idioms

The two idioms of the book, that of the courtiers and that of the narrator, create a tension between each other; and both of them are crucial for the discourse of the book. Neither is dominant, as they actually constitute a single entity. Such dialectics is necessary for the book, necessary to lay bare the mechanisms of power. Let us take a closer look at both idioms.

Kapuściński creates the language of the courtiers in such a way that it generates a picture of a caustic, conservative, old-fashioned place. It resembles the structure of Haile Selassie's court – it is as stern and rigid, as the court was and adhering to its principles. The language of the courtiers sounds old, archaic. Their sentences are long, sometimes half a page long. They often use archaic, Latin-based syntax – verbs are placed at the end of sentences. The courtiers use elaborate metaphors, flowery epithets, biblical vocabulary, exalted similes: "A kiedy się najedli, wytańczyli, pana swojego chwalili."[56] ("When they had guzzled and gamboled, they gave praise to their King" 99). As a counterbalance to this archaic, flowery language of the courtiers, the narrator speaks using a simple, headline-news-type of idiom. His sentences are short, his words are harsh, almost jarring, there are no flowery ornaments, no archaisms. His vocabulary is contemporary; it seems that he insists on separating himself from the court's baroque dialect.

Occasionally, the narrator interjects a little bit of his own narration.[57] He similarly interrupts other stories of the courtiers; he does it separately from his longer narratives. These little interjections are the narrator's accounts of what was happening with his interlocutors during the course of the described events. This part of text is always italicized, just like the nar-

---

56 Z.S.-K's story, page 94 of the Polish edition.
57 P.H-T's story, page 51 of the Polish edition.

rator's own, more typical, longer accounts of Haile Sellasie's decline and fall. These italicized interjections break the text, cut into its smooth flow. They create an effect of a crack on a seemingly perfect surface. The archaic, pathetic and smooth language of the courtiers gets broken, moved, undermined by the italicized interjections.

Yet, in spite of the obvious differences, both idioms create one language, one discourse of the book. They both describe the same thing; only they employ various strategies. They both describe the court, the tyranny, the atrocities, the last year of Haile Selassie's reign. However, while the courtiers seemingly worship and praise the emperor to high heavens, in their stories they actually lay bare the emperor's ruthlessness, the ugly mechanisms of corruption, thievish division of goods, cajolery, fraud, stealing and deception. At the same time, the narrator is the only person who speaks about the tyrant without this appalling, sugar-coated adulation, and is the only one capable of seeing him as an aging and lonely person.

The phenomenal present in reportage helps resist crude generalizations and causes reportage to never be omniscient. In *The Emperor,* the phenomenal is strongly present: both sides of the discourse are extremely personal and very subjective. They both show the court and the tyranny only from their own perspective and do not take into consideration either the 'objective' view of things or the other side's opinion.

It is the subjective aspect of both sides of the discourse that makes the book strong. The factual side only powerfully reinforces the phenomenal basis. *The Emperor* undoubtedly contains a vast number of verifiable facts; however, it also contains many utterly silly stories of no genuine importance (for instance a story about a courtier whose sole responsibility was to wipe the emperor's dog's urine off the dignitaries' shoes). Such insignificant facts only when gathered together and placed in the context of the book acquire meaning (similarly to a sign in Ferdinand de Saussure's model of language), that is they describe the palace's tyrannical system.[58]

The last paragraph of the narrator's introduction to the book (shortly before the beginning of Chapter 1 – "Throne") both semantically and symbolically anticipates the events of the book's narrative:

„Niepotrzebnie powtarzają, abym uważał: żadnych adresów ani nazwisk, ani nawet opisywać twarzy, ani że wysoki, że niski, że chudy; czoło jakie, że ręce mu, że spojrzenie, a nogi to, kolana, już nie ma przed kim na kolanach."[59]

---

58 Ferdinand de Saussure, *Writings in General Linguistics*, Oxford: Oxford University Press, 2006.
59 Page 10 of the Polish edtion.

„They caution me again, needlessly: no addresses, no names, don't say that he's tall, that he's short, that he's skinny, that his forehead this or that his hands that. Or that his eyes, or that is legs, or that his knees... There is nobody let to get down on your knees for," 5). This iconoclasm is necessary to set the stage as it anticipates the courtiers' fear of Haile Selassie's inconsequentiality. The last fragment of the sentence is very telling in Polish: „[...] że ręce mu, że spojrzenie, a nogi to, kolana, już nie ma przed kim na kolanach." Kapuściński skillfully creates an impression that he simply recorded what people told him: people whose language is quite colloquial, who at first are extremely cautious and terrified of what might happen to them, but quickly decide they do not care anymore. It sounds like an old person who knows very well that no one is really listening, so he does not even finish what he was going to say. "[J]uż nie ma przed kim na kolanach" – it does not quite sound like a sly narrator of a sophisticated book about terrifying mechanisms of power, rather it sounds more like my late grandmother. The English does not quite render it, as the translators decided to change this particular phrase into a grammatically correct sentence: "There's nobody left to get down on your knees for." The English sentence too sounds colloquial, but there is no feeling of this complete collapse present at the end of the long Polish sentence fragment. In the original there is a significant and sudden disintegration of syntax, signaling what is going to happen later in the narrative – how the court, the palace, the system of power are going to crumble. The breakdown is unexpected, happening during the time of the utterance, just like the dissolution of the court. This one sentence portrays the entire process of the monarchy's disintegration: from the despotic "no names, no addresses," through details, to a complete and sudden collapse "już nie ma przed kim na kolanach" – as if the supporting structure of the syntax (and of the court) abruptly stopped existing.

Kapuściński throughout the entire book tackles two opposing idioms, that of the courtiers and that of the narrator (not to be confused with the author), without letting either of them get the upper hand in the conflict. The result is a book with a strong opposition of two sides of the discourse, which are firmly tied one to another and cannot exist one without another. However, the tension between them, the dialectical split constitutes a third element, equally indispensable. All three elements are controlled by the narrator in a skillful and precise way.

2. Fabric of language

The book is constructed with a mathematical precision. The structure is symmetric, divided into three equal parts: introduction consisting of two pages of quotations, 50 pages of the first chapter, two pages of quotations, 50 pages of the second chapter, two pages of quotations, 50 pages of the third chapter, and an epilogue. The version of the book from 1978 is 150 pages long, and so is my version from 1988. The font and layout could be easily squeezed to make a shorter book, but they are not. The form is so precise, so rigid, that it might bring to mind the Ethiopian court: caustic, static, fixed. And just like the court in 1974, the book at the end just collapses. The Ethiopian court under the reign of Haile Sellasie had a precisely defined structure and hierarchy, yet ultimately it just crumbled under its own weight. Similarly, the discourse of the book is always on the brink of collapse, which finally occurs at the end of the book.

Kapuściński has a particular way of proving that he is in full control of the language of his characters – he bends and mutilates it, digs up unusual forms, creates neologisms. Kapuściński masterfully employs complicated and precise Polish grammar and exploits many traits of the Polish language, such as when a grammatical form carries a semantic connotation (an example of this trait can be seen in attaching a non-virile ending to virile plural noun forms with the intention of being offensive, i.e. "doktory," instead of "doktorzy"). He conveys a specific mood or a situation employing grammatical mimesis. For instance, when describing the court – static, rigid, caustic – he accumulates nouns; when he writes about the rebellion – tumultuous and energetic – we see a compilation of verbs.

A courtier with the initials F.U.H., talks about he intrigues undertaken by members of the court in order to ascend in the system and especially to be part of Ethiopia's delegations to foreign lands. Apparently, going abroad was a chance to get rich.[60] Kapuściński expertly conveys the palace's maneuvering through a collection of verbal nouns: "rozkopywanie, wywracanie, przesuwanie, wyprzedzanie." ("pushing and undermining, and elbowing" 61).

Several lines down: "W pałacu wrzenie, zaślepienie, po korytarzach bieganie, koterii naradzanie..." ("In the Palace there was agitation, obsession, running back and forth through the corridors. Coteries conferred..." 61).

Nouns denote objects, situations, feelings, but they do not signify action. They are static, they portray things, but they do not set things into motion. Nouns are preservative, immobile, which is the kind of impression one gets from reading this fragment: the courtiers do a lot to conserve their status quo, they run around the palace, they pretend to do something useful and worthy, but the real outcome of it is nothing. Nothing really changes in the country, only their positions within the court.

---

60 Page 62 of the Polish edition.

F.U.H continues with his story, and we again see an accumulation of verbal nouns: "ucztowanie, nabywanie, obławianie,"[61] ("abundant feasts, much buying and the chance to stuff a bundle of cash into one's pockets" 62) which conveys a caustic atmosphere mixed with desperate and pathetic greed. Another courtier named P.M. tells a story of a certain negativity that fell upon the court after the bloody suppression of a peasant uprising in 1960. The fact that Haile Selassie could actually be defied made a crack in the seemingly perfect life of the court. In the description of the 'negativity,' which appeared in the life of the court, Kapuściński again shows his brilliant craft: "była minusowość, w tym, co mówili nie mówiąc, w ich byciu nieobecnym, skurczonym, wyłączonym, w ich istnieniu wygaszonym, w ich myśleniu krótkodystansowym, niskopoprzeczkowym, w ich dłubaniu przyzagrodowym, malopoletkowym, w ich zapuszczeniu i zaćmieniu" ("there was negativism in what they said without speaking; in their absent being, as is shrunken, switched off; in their burnt-out existence; in their short-range, small-stuff thinking; in their vegetable-patch, cottage garden digging; in their weed-grown, overcast look" 82). The fragment is a series of long, combined adjectives, which all rhyme with each other. The repetition of similarly sounding adjectives gives this fragment a feeling of things being static and repetitive.

The syntax used in P.M.'s story is as archaic as this character's mindset. The lexicon Kapuściński uses is incredible in its abundance and variety. Kapuściński was famous for spending weeks, even months just on reading, most often belle lettres, after coming back from his travels and before he even took a pen in his hand to begin writing a new book. He claimed that after months spent abroad and of functioning in a foreign language he had to 'refresh' his Polish through submerging himself in Polish literature. This strategy is evident in this particular fragment, which contains a rich vocabulary characteristic for the Baroque or the Enlightenment periods – an old-fashioned lexicon and word morphology: "głowę podnosić, horrenda różne gadać, nierozumnie i jakże obelżywie przeciw pałacowi występować. Młodziankowie ci, miast za dobrodziejstwa oświaty wdzięczność okazywać, puścili się na mętne i zdradliwe wody obmowy i wichrzenia."[62] ("[they] had started to raise their heads more and more, to tell horrendous stories, and to speak unreasonably and insultingly against the palace. Instead of showing their gratitude for the benefits of enlightenment, those youngsters launched themselves on the turbid and treacherous waters of slander and faction" 87).

Even the mere fact of placing the verbs at the end of each clause makes the story sound old, detached from reality. Sentences are very long and stretch for as much as twelve lines. This character has an archaic way of expressing himself,

---

61   Page 63 of the Polish edition.
62   Page 83 of the Polish edition.

therefore it should not come as a surprise that he sticks to the old order, supports the emperor and opposes the students in their fight for changes. Each word, the word order, even the words' archaic morphology used by this person say: oldness, stagnation, preservation. Kapuściński creates a character who, even after the system's collapse and the revelation of its atrocities and monstrous crimes, still talks about the greatness of it.

A courtier hiding under the abbreviation M. begins his story by addressing his interviewer as "łaskawca" ("my friend" in the translation), which sounds archaic and evokes a feeling of adulation.[63] M. talks about an uprising organized in 1968 by the Ethiopian farmers against monstrous bureaucracy and against a sudden surge of taxes that were introduced to support that bureaucracy. The palace had been convinced that the Ethiopian nation was appeased by reforms, which the court advertised widely, even though the courtiers knew very well the reforms did not change anything. To the great surprise of the palace, people were not fooled by the advertisements and appearances. The uprising came as a shock, since the simple folk in Ethiopia, before the uprising, had lived in a feudal tradition of humility and subjection of the lower classes toward the higher ones. In 1968 college students joined the farmers in their rebellion and openly accused the palace of all the atrocities. In spite of their combined efforts, the rebellion was quickly and bloodily silenced. In the part of the story where M. describes the peasants rebelling and then students joining the rebellion, Kapuściński accumulates many verbs, often in one sentence: "...[c]hłopi warcholą, burzą się, kwestorom czaszki łupią, wieszają policjantów, gonią notabli, palą dwory, niszczą zbiory... buntownicy szturmują urzędy... lżą, katują, ćwiartują... [A] w stolicy już studenci występują, buntowników chwalą, palcem dwór wytykają, kalumnie ciskają."[64] ("...[t]he peasants are brawling, rebelling, bashing the skulls of tax collectors, hanging policemen, running dignitaries out of town, burning down estates, uprooting crops... rebels are storming the offices... they vilify them, torture them, and quarter them... And in the capital the students defend the rebels, praising them, pointing their finger at the court, hurling insults" 96). Verbs signify action, energy, things happening here and now. In the text, the rebelling peasants and the revolting students are associated with verbs. There are few nouns in this fragment, since nouns are associated with the palace. In English it is the present continuous tense – the '-ing' forms – that give it a feeling of things happening, rapidity and fierceness. Kapuściński skillfully and precisely uses grammar to convey the feeling of fear slowly overtaking the palace and the fierceness of the opposition movement.

---

63 Pages 89-90 of the Polish edition.
64 Page 91 of the Polish edition.

3. Situational schizophrenia – two languages

Society existing under a tyrannical rule develops a certain type of situational schizophrenia, since it has to function in two realities at once – in the unsafe and unstable reality of the official world and in the more or less safe world of the private, domestic life. A courtier with the initials P.M. develops this thought further by talking about the Ethiopian society simultaneously using two languages – the official, which was smooth, nice and praising the system and the private – cracked, bitter and cynical (89). The society has to employ a technique of a certain dissimulation of power so as to live more intimately in the everyday, and consequently the first to suffer under any tyranny is language.[65]

In the midst of the text, a Polish reader sees a familiar phrase: "...pełno zbójców na drodze..." weaved into the story told by a courtier named A.A.[66] The line comes from an Adam Mickiewicz's poem titled "Powrót taty" published in 1822 in Vilnius and known to virtually every Polish reader. Seeing this Romantic poetry phrase in the middle of a factual story told at the end of the 20th century by an Ethiopian courtier about a collapse of a regime in a small country in Africa creates an unusual feeling. What is this phrase doing in this book? Did Kapuściński use it to 'defamiliarize' us with the text, to use the term coined by Victor Shklovsky? It seems that we are being reminded about the inherent fictionality of this text. It is rather obvious that an Ethiopian courtier did not quote Mickiewicz, when talking about a dangerous situation on the roads in far provinces. For some reason, however, Kapuściński thought it would be fitting to use a quotation from a 19th century Polish Romantic poet. The phrase is not separated by quotation marks; neither does it stand out in any way from the rest of the text. How fictive then is this text? Where does fiction begin? How much creation is there here?

According to Lisa Wedeen, in contemporary times, there is no 'true' authoritarianism; instead, there is only 'low cost' authoritarianism, a bit ineffective, a little cheap, postmodern version of the grand old totalitarian systems. In order for such low cost authoritarianism to survive, both the holders of power and the ruled masses are required to act "as if." The power equation necessitates both sides to pretend that they accept the power structure as true, but no one actually believes in it: "the regime demands that citizens provide external evidence of their allegiance to a cult whose rituals of adulation are manifestly unbelievable."[67] Maybe Selassie was the last old-fashioned totalitarian ruler of modern times, such who believed in his own greatness.

---

65 Lisa Wedeen, *Ambiguities of Domination: Politics, Rhetoric, and Symbols in Contemporary Syria*, Chicago: University of Chicago Press, 1999, p. 80.
66 Page 106 of the Polish edition.
67 Wedeen, *Ambiguities…*, p. 62.

His courtiers, however, did not. His courtiers, the creators and supporters of the palace language, were cynics, as defined by Slavoj Žižek.

An authoritarian system, such as Hafez Assad's cult in Syria described by Weeden, is equally responsible for generating power, but also for inviting into it a certain type of instability – the instability of language. Scholars of oppression, for instance Tejumola Olaniyan, have argued that both the ruler and the ruled are "locked inextricably in the tyranny of language,"[68] but in my opinion in *The Emperor* each act of transgression shows the "disposition of language to undermine its own authorizing logic."[69] The stronger the opposition in Ethiopia and the more atrocities there are to hide, the more Baroque, flowery and ornamental the palace language becomes. And so it goes until the moment of a complete collapse, that is until the end of Selassie's regime. The conceptual and symbolic system of language is destabilized by a totalitarian system and sooner or later it has to bring an outcome. The palace rhetoric cannot exist on its own, so it quickly dies together with the system it praises.

---

68 Tejumola Olaniyan, "Narrativizing Postcoloniality: Responsibilities," *Public Culture* 5:1 (Fall 1992): 50.
69 Wedeen, *Ambiguities...*, p. 85.

II. Characters vs. Discourse

The characters in the book are created in such way that they function as critics of the flaws and atrocities of the system while seemingly praising it to high heavens. They rarely use irony in their stories – they do not distance themselves from the events or from the court. There is a feeling of total association of the characters with the palace and with the emperor. However, when ostensibly admiring the palace, they actually reveal all the flaws of the system. It is from their stories that we learn out about all the atrocities, frauds, backwardness, murders, ethnic cleansings, starvation. The narrator serves as a counterbalance to the lofty, bombastic and yet pathetic tone, which they set, but most of the information actually comes from them.

The first story of the book (by F.) is told in a serious manner, as are most of the stories; there is not even a shadow of irony or humor in his narrative, even though his story is actually quite comical. The courtier talks about his position at the court, which he held for more than ten years. His only responsibility was to wipe off the Emperor's lap dog's urine, in case the dog urinated on dignitiaries' shoes during official audiences or meetings at the palace. F. never points out the ridiculousness or the sheer repulsiveness of his 'work,' nor does he try to explain himself; he calmly and dispassionately relates the story of his job for ten years. Whether he willingly subjected himself to humiliation in front of hundreds of people, just so he could be part of the elite, is seemingly left for the reader to determine. In the story, F. never mentions any attempts to searching for a different job or to change his life. The character is created in such a way that we *have* to conclude that he was willing to be human toilet paper and that the only reward for his disgrace was to be close to the ones who divided the goods.

Kapuściński opens up the book with F's story. The reader is then immediately thrown into the grotesque, psychotic and scary atmosphere of the late years of Haile Selassie's tyranny. The atmosphere resembles the tales told about Stalin's "court" or Suetonius's descriptions of the lives of Roman emperors.[70] Moreover, the reader is also instantaneously lead to thinking how the treacherous methods of power and influence unavoidably corrupt people.

A character with the initials T.L. describes Haile Selassie's method of selecting his ministers from people who were young, energetic, but not too smart, from lower classes and often living in extreme poverty.[71] They always became his greatest fans, his most fierce supporters. Those ministers realized their entire careers depended on Haile Selassie's whims and moods, so they served him with

---

70   Tranquillus Gaius Suetonius, *The Twelves Ceasars*, New York: Penguin, 2000.
71   Page 32 of the Polish edition.

passion. We are told straightforwardly by T.L. that Selassie did not have much formal education, but the reader is left to conclude that the emperor used cunning and intelligent methods of manipulating and ruling people around him. The same topic continues further in the book, in P.H.-T's story.[72] Selassie was protective of his unintelligent ministers, as they provided the stabilizing element for the totalitarian structure. He kept those ministers close so they could issue idiotic laws, decrees and bills, which later educated young people tried to upend. Through such methods, the energy of those young people was not directed at overturning the monarchy and the balance of this whole dysfunctional system was maintained.

As we read further, a courtier G.O.E. explains Haile Selassie's strategy of selecting new servants undertaken after the 1968 peasant uprising.[73] The monarch brought simple, uneducated people from the farthest provinces into the palace; these were people who knew no history and who had never even heard of the uprising, since the emperor banned history books from Ethiopia. G.O.E. reveals Haile Sellasie's entire process of rising to power through a conspiracy and his broken promise to protect Ethiopia from foreign, mainly Italian, invaders (when the Italians actually invaded, the emperor went to England and spent the entire war there). Therefore, G.O.E. reveals Selassie's many lies, intrigues and scams, while seemingly constantly praising the emperor.

A courtier named B. H. clarifies the division of the country's budget in the late 1960s. At that time in Ethiopia, there were approximately 30 million farmers and about a hundred thousand soldiers and policemen. The farmers received 1% of the state budget and the military and the police 40% of it. Through such statements, the atrocities and injustices of the system are laid bare, even though the character seems to not intend to reveal any faults of the late period of the autocratic system. Later in his story, B.H. attempts to excuse Selassie for not knowing what went on behind the walls of the palace, in the 'real' world, and that the innocent emperor's lack of knowledge (and not his conscious evil will) brought serious consequences on everyone tied with the court. Such thinking is a *classic* way of absolving a tyrant of his sins by his subjects – maintaining the tyrant was innocent, even though in reality he was clearly the one guilty of the crimes of the system. So is B.H. trying to blame Selassie (though revealing the atrocities) or absolving him (through upholding his faith in Selassie's innocence)? Or both?

Much later in the text, in a fragment with the heading "June-July," a courtier named U.Z.W., talks about river dams that Selassie wanted to build on the

---

72   *Ibid*, p. 50.
73   *Ibid*, p. 77.

Nile.[74] The narrator claims that military officers who were conspiring against Selassie, instead tried to push for spending the money on feeding the hungry, as he clearly supports the change that the officers paid by the Soviet Union were about to bring to the country. The emperor of course preferred a dam, since that would be a monument built to glorify his name for ages, while the hungry would die anyway. Even when it was already clear that his doom was approaching, in the words of the narrator, Selassie did not give up thoughts and actions praising his own greatness. The language U.Z.W. uses is again archaic and lofty; he even has rhymed slogans praising the emperor: "zaś potwarca niech knuje, szczuje – rozwoju tam nie zatamuje! ... chyba tylko sam cesarz zdolen był takie niezwykłości powznosić, góry całe w poprzek ustawić!" ("Let the slanderers spew their lies and shams – they will suffer in hell for opposing our dams! [...] Who but the Emperor cold have caused such things to be done, such extraordinary, wondrous things, whole mountains flung across the river!").

A character named Y.Y. tells a story of the plans that the officers had concerning the future of Selassie.[75] The scary, paralyzing change was coming, and it is reflected by a slow change in the text. The shadow of change is constantly cast over the palace, the revolution is inevitable. According to Y.Y., there was, however, a faction in the palace, which did not acknowledge reality and wanted Selassie to maintain his absolute monarchy, even when the officers were in fact already ruling the country. In the meantime, the palace's connection with reality was becoming weaker and weaker; Y.Y. talks about not knowing which of the two worlds – palace vs. the rest – was actually real.

Further into the book, another courtier E., talks about the inevitable transformations, which were drawing near the palace. In this fragment, the language becomes more regular – no archaisms, no flowery language, no Latin-based syntax; instead the language is dry, concrete, down to the point. As if the palace rhetoric were dying together with the palace... Toward the end of the book, in T.W's story, we see another switch in the courtiers' language; this time it is a language of a very simple person, of a lower-ranking servant – as if the narrator was running out of people whom he could interview. The closer we are to the collapse of the tyranny, and together with that – to the end of the book, the simpler the language becomes. The collapse of the palace is reflected closely by the change in the book's discourse, even the sequence of events in the book mirrors the chronology of events in reality. The discourse of the palace collapses as the book nears its end.

---

74 Page 122 of the Polish edition.
75 Page 138 of the Polish edition.

At first sight, there is not even a tiny bit of irony in the courtiers' stories. The courtiers are completely serious (after all, laughter and irony, as many discovered a long time ago, are the first to suffer under tyranny; but that is a completely different story). The structure of the courtiers' narratives presents them as direct speech: the first person narration, colloquial language and grammar, and trivial details. Yet, the reader has to remain aware that what we see in the book are characters, not quotations from someone's actual everyday speech. Kapuściński creates the characters, basing their story very loosely on his notes, impressions and memories. This is not a traditionally understood reporting, which is based on a temporal and spatial immediacy of events and on the verifiability of the facts. The discourse of this book is a created (that is ironic, or distanced) discourse lacking irony (that is irony-less or non-ironic). The discourse is based on a discord, as there is a split, a dialectical divide at the very base of it. Its constitution peculiarly reflects what it describes: a fictional discourse based very loosely on the facts. The book is built on a created discourse that describes a political system that similarly claimed not to be created – a fictional discourse with aspirations to being non-fiction (the people of Ethiopia were told the court and the power of the emperor were not created; they were 'given from above,' Haile Selassie even had Ethiopia's constitution changed so it would say he was a descendant of King Salomon). The book's discourse then resembles the Ethiopian autocratic system, which was fictional (and fictive) and aspired to be taken as real. Just like the fictive system it describes, the book's discourse simply disintegrates – the book ends without a conclusion.

4. Comfortable status quo

The characters-courtiers are followers, not leaders, or creators. Selassie chose his courtiers very carefully; they had to be opportunistic, cowardly, petty, narrow-minded. He rarely made the mistake of choosing someone brave, open-minded and courageous. The narrator says openly that in an autocratic system it is always the autocrat who is solely responsible for the meanness and pettiness of his functionaries. The courtiers do not do anything to change their convenient and comfortable status quo, even when they know that they benefit (and benefit greatly) from oppression, hunger and extreme poverty of the masses. They never take the path, which Oedipus took after he had realized his crimes, that is publicly admitting to his mistakes and taking responsibility for them. They desperately cling to the emperor, they are willing to be offended, humiliated, do utterly ridiculous jobs as long as they are close to the division of goods and privileges.

In *The Sublime Object of Ideology* Slavoj Žižek explains an approach to reality based on 'cynical reason.' He famously writes that cynicism is just another "way to (willingly) blind ourselves to the structuring power of ideological fantasy: even if we do not take things seriously, even if we keep an ironical distance, we are still doing them... 'they [people blinding themselves to ideology and yet benefiting from the division of goods] know that, in their activity, they are following an illusion, but still, they are doing it.'"[76] Another aspect of the cynical reason is remembering that "the real obedience is an 'external' one," as the real obedience relies on not believing in the power structure (since obedience out of conviction would mean having judgment; obedience is *not* judgment). Such was the method of functioning of the courtiers – consciously blinding themselves to the fact that the Sellasie's regime was used for ruthless and long-termed exploitation of the Ethiopian nation. Kapuściński shows the courtiers as cynical exploiters of the system, who ran as quickly as possible the moment the system started to crumble.

Kapuściński, similarly to Žižek, seems to be convinced that the Marxian naïve view of ideology "Sie wissen das nicht, aber sie es tun – the do not know it, but they are doing it"[77] is now only an illusion. He is convinced that in a tyrannical system, people close to the ruler always are well aware of all the shortcomings of the system, yet they choose to not see them and to take advantage of them in every possible way. Interestingly enough, this calm and reserved take on ideology provides evidence to a more or less decisive Kapuściński's farewell to his own youthful and naïve worldview formed by post-war Polish socialism.

---

76 Slavoj Žižek, *The Sublime Object of Ideology*, London, New York: Verso, 1999, p. 33.
77 Karl Marx, *Capital,* after Žižek, *The Sublime...*, p. 28.

III. Power

Many analyses of *The Emperor* call it an in-depth study of power – an indirect analysis of tyrannical power, its enormous ability to corrupt and damage, and of cynical exploitation of an abnormal system by ruthless people. Critics of the book often see it as an allegory of the vast authority and control the Communist Party held over Poland in the late 1970s. The most famous of such analyses is Carl Tighe's "Ryszard Kapuściński and *The Emperor*."[78] Tighe writes:

> It is clear that *The Emperor* maybe also be read as a commentary on what was happening in Poland... Polish readers saw in the Emperor's patronage both the massive powers of the First Secretary of the PZPR and appointments made to keep official position, the *nomenklatura*... The spirit that informs the work, the details that the author thinks worthy of note, the sense of circumstance and history, of cultural specifics all have their roots in the typically Polish game of hunt the Symbol, in the business of talking about Poland while ostensibly talking about something entirely different.

While I am not going to negate this claim, I think that it is a disservice to the book to say it is *only* that; I am convinced that there are many significant aspects of the book that do not pertain to the structure of power and to methods of its functioning. Having said that, I agree that power and closely tied to it – ideology – have a strong presence in *The Emperor*, and I am going to dedicate some time to examining them.

Žižek says:

> What we call 'social reality' is in the last resort an ethical construction; it is supported by a certain *as if* (we act *as if* we believe in the almightiness of bureaucracy, *as if* the President incarnates the Will of the People, *as if* the Party expresses the objective interest of the working class...). As soon as the belief (which, let us remind ourselves again, is definitely not to be conceived at a 'psychological' level: it is embodied, materialized, in the effective functioning of the social field) is lost, the very texture of the social field disintegrates.[79]

In other words: even though belief in authority is external (which is counterintuitive, as we are used to thinking about belief as an internal process), in the sense that it is embodied in *practice*, in the very functioning of society, and through that functioning, through that practice, it imposes itself on us (hence its externality). More importantly though, reciprocity is *absolutely necessary* for authority to exist. The moment reciprocity ceases to exist, authority collapses.

---

78 Tighe, "Ryszard Kapuściński and..."
79 *The Sublime...*, p. 33.

A courtier named W.A-N., says "A przecież władza nie może pracować w klimacie zagrożenia, władza to jest pewna umowność oparta na ustalonych regułach." (Government can't work under threat, can it? Isn't government a convention, based on established rules?)[80] Power and authority, like other social conventions, are just an agreement. And just like with any other social convention, people have to agree to (or be forced to) participate in it, they have to accept the rules of it. More than that – they have to provide a conducive atmosphere for it to grow ("[...] władza nie może pracować w klimacie zagrożenia [...]") Authority requires support both from its subjects and its creators.

W.A.N. continues the argument for the reciprocity of authority by telling a story of the emperor expressing a wish to visit simple country folk. The court, always eager to fulfill its ruler's wishes, had to arrange everything beforehand, so the monarch's visit would maintain a proper royal grandness. The courtiers had to educate the local people about the imperial visitor they were going to see and how they were required to behave, since villagers from far corners of Ethiopia were often not even cognizant of the fact that they were the emperor's subjects. After that, the courtiers had to bring in it more educated people from bigger towns, so Selassie would be greeted properly. The courtiers had to tell the locals to clean their huts, to dress appropriately, to sweep the pathways, to hide the sick and the old from sight, etc. (all practices familiar to people raised on the east side of the Iron Curtain). If all of that were not arranged and not carefully prepared, if Selassie's visits were truly unexpected, he might have had to face people who did not know who he was. His throne would be standing in the desert and there would be no one bowing to him, no one paying him respect. There would be just his throne, him and the desert. There would be *no one recognizing his power*, and *that* would be the ultimate absurd and nonsense for W.A.N: the emperor cannot be unrecognized, since his authority is solely funded in reciprocity of the power relation.

Power does not exist without audience. It is a convention, an interaction into which we enter or are forced to enter. However, where does the theatricality of power stop and where does reality begin? How far can the political *teatrum absurdum* go? Are the limits of theatricality defined by the presence of an actual, breathing, and hopefully not bleeding body? Most tyrants are not concerned with live, breathing people, tyrants actually want bodies, they want the reciprocity of power to be based on fear of losing one's life, rather than respect and cooperation.

Without an audience, there would be a throne in a desert or presidential candidates without the voters. The assumption of power (the assumption being the

---

80 Page 40 of the English language edition.

presence of subjects) would be undermined, and the absurdity of such situation would be more dangerous to any authority than a violent uprising.

> I met a traveler from an antique land
> Who said: Two vast and trunkless legs of stone
> Stand in the desert. Near them, on the sand,
> Half sunk, a shattered visage lies, whose frown
> And wrinkled lip, and sneer of cold command
> Tell that its sculptor well those passions read
> Which yet survive, stamped on these lifeless things,
> The hand that mocked them and the heart that fed.
> And on the pedestal these words appear:
> "My name is Ozymandias, king of kings:
> Look on my works, ye Mighty, and despair!"
> Nothing beside remains. Round the decay
> Of that colossal wreck, boundless and bare
> The lone and level sands stretch far away.
>
> (Ozymandias, Percy Bysshe Shelley)

The theme of the theatricality of power is carried on by another courtier named E.; he reflects on the conventionality of power.[81] Whenever Haile Selassie traveled, immediately after his departure his palace turned into a mock-up, into a prop. Without the emperor, the palace ceased to be a foreign object in Ethiopia's body, it suddenly was internalized by the surroundings; it became an integral part of the country: there was laundry drying on ropes, the cattle were grazing on the lawn, the gates were chained together, the palace servants cooked outside and slept under the trees. The main prop (or the main actor), Selassie, had to be present there in order for the palace to function as his stage, the moment he left the palace ceased to be a theatrical set.

Toward the end of the book, we read a story about the last months of Sellasie's reign told by a courtier named A.G. The emperor "would comfort them, wish them success, attach the greatest importance, treat them with personal care [...]"[82] – all these words of comfort and wishes of success were uttered by an emperor, who was about to be forced to abdicate, toward soldiers, who were the ones forcing him to abdication. Whenever the soldiers entered the palace (during the last months no one invaded the palace, soldiers just entered it at will), the emperor directed his tirades at them. It is a truism to say that interaction is crucial for meaning. Only the presence of an interlocutor allows for the meaning of words or of a ceremonial (which is, after all, only another means of communication) to come into existence. Selassie was aware of that and until the last mo-

---

81 Page 43 of the Polish edition.
82 Page 136 of the Polish edition.

ment he wanted to determine the direction of the discourse of the country, or at least of the palace was going. He needed the other person for the dialogue to exist, but he still wanted to be the one managing the conversation. However, at that point in time, his words, all that "comfort, importance, care" had already lost their meaning, since his audience was no longer his. His erstwhile loyal and eager listeners were no longer paying attention; they were not engaged in an exchange of any kind. The 'dialogue' was only his illusion.

The moment authority is ignored, it dies.

IV. The narrator

Even though the book is entitled *The Emperor*, the actual emperor never appears in the book directly in person. Selassie never speaks directly, is never quoted, never directly addresses the courtiers. His terrifying shadow is constantly cast over the courtiers' memories, but the reader never meets him in person. The book is *about* him, but *without* him. He is an absent presence. There is, however, another stern power structure upholder lurking between the lines of the book. It is the narrator. A mysterious and ominous ruler, the narrator guards the book's realm and watches that the book's hierarchy is upheld; he rules the book's discourse with an iron hand, resembling in his strict approach the tyrant from the book's title. He brings up or breaks up the courtiers' stories whenever he sees fit, cuts the courtiers short, ridicules them, punishes them, and at the end, sends them into oblivion. He lets them be or not. He explains the palace events as if he held the monopoly on truth – he knows everything and has seen everything. His position within the book is well thought through (he makes sure his presence in the discourse is absolutely necessary, he convinces the reader that someone has to take upon himself to expose and balance the ridiculousness and smarminess of the petty courtiers). It is almost as if he had to secure his place within the narrative and guarantee that his status would not be questioned by anyone in the book.

No character ever inquires about his position, no one directs any questions at him; he is the only one allowed to ask and to report back to the reader. And not just that, he also uses various methods to shape the book's discourse to his liking and to facilitate or simplify his task.

5. The narrator – collector of memories

The narrator breaks his own rule far into the book and for the first and only time reveals the name of his interlocutor.[83] The courtier's name was Teferra, and he agreed to help the narrator find the emperor's former entourage: „Byliśmy parą kolekcjonerów pragnących odzyskać skazane na zniszczenie obrazy, aby zrobić z nich wystawę dawnej sztuki władania."[84] ("We were a couple of collectors out to recover pictures doomed to destruction: we wanted to make an exhibition of the old art of governing" 23).

Teferra and the narrator decided to create an exhibit of an age-old art of domination and supremacy. Through a powerful tool of language and by placing

---

83 Page 26 of the Polish edition.
84 Page 26 of the Polish edition.

the events in the brackets of the past, the narrator and Teferra canonized the actual events and real people, and turned them into museum artifacts, exhibition objects. An art exhibit, or a painting collection, does not contain live organisms (most of them, at least), can be more or less easily described, can be defined. It is much easier to talk about, write about something that does not exist anymore, something conveniently bracketed by the past. "Museumizing" the facts made the narrator's job much easier. It was much easier for the narrator to talk about the past events and inconsequential people rather than to relate the newest events and facts from lives of people currently alive. Assuming a safe temporal distance not only made the narrator's job easier but also allowed to him to "customize" the facts in a way that fit his version of the story.

6. Narrator folds time

At the beginning of a book, when everything in Selassie's court seems to function perfectly and according to the emperor's meticulous plan, the narrator unexpectedly folds time and goes into the future of the story – he says that the first question directed straightforwardly to the emperor (as no one had done it before) was a sign of the upcoming revolution. We have to keep in mind that until the early 1970s, in Selassie's palace, questions were asked only from the top down. Then the narrator corrects himself (as if he forgot himself for a second and let himself go into the future), goes back to the chronological order of the book and tells a story of the emperor's morning ritual of feeding the caged lions, leopards and other predators, which took place for more than several decades in an unchanged form, until 1974. While the emperor wanted to rule over time and to keep it still by repeating the same rituals for months, years and even decades, the narrator conversely shows his power over time – he folds it, jumps between the past, present and future.

Most of the narrators' fragments are rendered in the present tense, while the stories of his interlocutors are almost always moved to the past tense. For the narrator the time and tenses do not exist, he is above them, he rules them. The courtiers rarely talk about the "future," they have a narrow perspective; they concentrate on the "now" of the events they describe. Contrary to them, the narrator moves around time and events freely, moreover, he is omniscient. He folds the fabric of the text however he pleases.

7. Narrator's auto-creation

Throughout the book, the narrator maintains his image as a careful and thoughtful participant of the local events. He never lets any information slip through the text's fabric that would undermine his image. Part of his image-creating technique is distancing himself from the rest of the foreign correspondents deployed to Ethiopia at that time. The narrator introduces a foreign correspondent of Turkish-Cyprish origin who wanted to complain to higher Ethiopian authorities how inefficiently the foreign correspondents' work was organized by the local bureaucrats. The narrator explains that the community of foreign correspondents consists of "cynical and tough people" who often do not care about the local population and do not comprehend the rules of the local reality, only about their reports being sent promptly. Had the Turkish correspondent actually decided to complain to some authorities, the courtier responsible for organizing the correspondents' work would face certain death – he most likely would be beheaded, says the narrator. The only person, out of all the reporters, who understood the danger looming over the incompetent courtier, was, of course, the narrator. And it was only after the narrator's intervention and much convincing that the Turk chose to remain quiet. Through such examples the narrator builds his carefully designed image.

The second chapter of the book, "It's Coming, It's Coming," brings descriptions of the unavoidable system transformation lining up on the horizon. The courtiers talk about the symptoms of decline with which life at the palace began to abound. The stories are told in a typical courtier fashion – with an unhurried pace, in a lofty language, one narrative smoothly following another. After approximately fifteen pages into the chapter of the courtiers' endless accounts, unexpectedly, the narrator jumps in with his own italicized typeface font and a completely different language. Dry, wry, almost ironic – the language of a distrustful and skeptical correspondent, who can easily see through the lies and masks of his interlocutors. Maintaining his persona, the narrator continually stresses the distance from the courtiers' stories by often repeating: "dalej mówi mi... dalej twierdzi... upiera się... wyznaje... wspomina..." ("He goes on to tell me... as my informant says... he insists... he confesses" 84). A little further, the narrator again interrupts his interviewees and describes with acute details the events of the 1968 uprising using a cold, dry language, which is different from the language of the courtiers. Reading this fragment brings almost a feeling of relief. After all these smarmy tales, the reader wants to be let out of that circle of slimy fawning. And the narrator, in a very skillful and calculated way, meets the reader's needs.

The narrator keeps his carefully calibrated distance from the events, but remains free to move between events and in time. Occasionally, he allows himself some humor or sarcasm, but even then his story remains tight and almost ascetic. He clarifies the reason behind the 1968 anti-palace insurgency's defeat.[85] Even though his explanation is trivial, it has a tragically comical element: the insurgents took over the city (or so they thought) and proclaimed their postulates over the radio waves. In 1968, Ethiopia was an extremely poor country and few people actually owned a radio. So the proclamation did not reach almost anyone and went nearly unnoticed. In the narrator's opinion then, in Ethiopia, at the end of the 1960's, things were pretty much the same as they were centuries ago. The 20th century had not reached that country yet.

8. The narrator anticipates the palace's collapse

At the end of the "It's Coming, It's Coming" chapter, in the last of the narrator's stories in this chapter, the narrator undertakes to explain the changes in the public's perception of Selassie at the end of the 1960s. The official image, promoted by the Palace in the Western media, was of a lucid, smart ruler, of a slowly but surely developing country, one who defied Mussolini and had ambitions to be an important world leader. The contradictory image was pushed by the opposition, and that one was of a ruthless tyrant, using all means to keep the status quo and to protect the stupidity, obtuseness, and servility of his court. The narrator claims that against all appearances, the emperor in fact understood that his palace was completely out of touch with reality, and that sooner or later it had to collapse. Despite that, the narrator says, Selassie did not change anything; on the contrary, the emperor maintained the status quo, as he himself was a hostage of a system that he created.

This narrator's story ends in a surprising way. He lists the features of Selassie's personality, such as "był wielce sympatyczną postacią, przenikliwym politykiem."[86] ("he was a most amiable personage, a shrewd politician" 102). And after that, just as the reader expects a more detailed analysis of Sellasie's personality, the grammar suddenly collapses, and the narrator almost nonchalantly says: "Ot, kaprysy władzy, labirynty polityki pałacowej, dwuznaczności, ciemności, nikt ich nie przeniknie." ("Whims of power, labyrinths of Palace politics, ambiguity, darkness that no one could penetrate"). The chapter actually ends in one last short story by a courtier named Z.S.-K. (which comes right after the narrator's un-finished fragment). Z.S.K. reminisces about the upcoming revolu-

---

85 Page 80 of the Polish edition.
86 Page 96 of the Polish edition.

tion, which was creeping toward the palace. The narrator does not conclude the chapter in any way. Why does he do it? Why does the grammar in his fragment simply disintegrate and the logic of this sentence collapse as well? Grammar provides the structure for language; hence the narrator starts to signal that together with the nearing collapse of the palace's configuration, the disintegration of its idiom is approaching.

At the end of the last chapter of the book, the narrator more and more often stresses that he was never influenced by the petty, servile mindset of the courtiers – in his narratives, which by the way become shorter and shorter the closer we are to the end, he sets things straight. His language is even harsher, meaner than earlier in the book; he is concrete to the point of obnoxiousness. The closer we are to the end of the book and to the fall of the emperor, the narrator interrupts the courtiers more and more as if he was encouraged by the crumbling palace, as if together with the upcoming overturn, he too gathers strength to talk. Earlier in the book, when the palace system is in good shape, the length of both the courtiers' and the narrator's stories is considerable, but at the end of the last third chapter, the events pick up pace and the characters and the narrator are only allowed speak fast and concisely.

The narrator is as much of a tyrant within the book's discourse as Selassie was in Ethiopia for many decades of his reign. While the word "tyrant" is usually burdened with negative associations, the tyrannical power of *The Emperor's* narrator should not be quickly rejected. He is the one who preserves the utterly precise structure of the book, he keeps the characters in place, he guards the carefully delineated border between the palace and is own metanarrative by constantly stressing the difference between the courtiers' idiom and his own idiom. Kapuściński then, through the persona of his narrator, subverts the uncomplicated aligning of power with evil, and once again rejects easy and quick labels.

V. The End (or lack thereof)

Toward the end of the book, the narrator tells a story of L.M., Selassie's personal butler. L.M. was of a similar age to the emperor and served Selassie until the final moment of the emperor's reign. On the last day of the monarchy, that is on September 12, 1974, the rebellious officers (at that point in time, "ruling" rather then "rebelling" would be a more fitting term) simply walked the elderly monarch to a car, and drove away. The equally old servant was told to pack his things and go home. Then, one of the remaining officers locked the palace, put the key in his pocket and everyone simply left. There was no one to defend Selassie (no one to attack him either), no one to throw stones or harsh words, there was no bloodshed. There was no pathos, no tragedy, no loftiness, as if a theatre play ended, and both the audience and the actors could finally go home.

I have written repeatedly that power requires reciprocity. Power has to demand mutuality from its participants, often has to fight for it. The narrator shows that it was just not the bloody uprisings, which deprived Selassie of his authority (the uprisings definitely contributed to the process), but it was the slow but steady process of the Ethiopians realizing that they were able to live its daily lives without the emperor and the palace pretending to run every aspect of it. The process, it should be noted, was sped-up tremendously by the pro-Soviet officers and their machinations supported to a great extent by the Soviet Union. In the second half of 1974, the process reached its completion, and Selassie was no longer significant or consequential to Ethiopia. Kapuściński captured the moment with an incredible clarity in the last scene of the book. The soon-to-become-former emperor was driven out of the palace, the palace was locked and no one even noticed that the erstwhile mighty emperor was not there anymore. This, in a way, was a worse ending to an autocratic regime than a violent revolution. The new government did not even deem Selassie dangerous; he was just taken to "safe isolated place," or so goes the official version of events.

It should be restated that Kapuściński wrote the book from a pro-Soviet stance. In no other book went Kapuściński that far in such a sweeping acceptance of a revolution, no matter how palatial it was. In no part of *The Emperor* does the author talk about the fact that the revolution destroyed one of the most fascinating and oldest forms of Christianity; instead the narrative concentrates on painting a prejudiced picture of a senile dotard who created a backwards system of which he himself is a prisoner. And he at the end – despite of the assurances given by Kapuściński in the book – is most likely executed.

The last scene of the old monarch obediently following the officers to a car and the old servant equally obediently leaving the palace in a complete silence, without any one else accompanying the emperor or without any angry, bloodthirsty crowds, with life in the streets of Addis Ababa going its course as if nothing happened is, in my opinion, one of the strongest and most moving in the book. It is heavy on symbolism and emotional load, and much more compelling than a scene with bloodshed, fighting, and violence. It is pathetic, in both meanings of the word: lofty and pitiable. The main text of the book ends on the scene of Haile Selassie being walked out of the palace and his servant locking the doors to it. No reflections or analyses follow the last scene, none of the usual narrator's revelations or conclusions; in fact neither the narrator nor any of the characters speak again. The ending of the book is symbolically similar to the end of the emperor's regime, with its lack of pathos at the end of Selassie's reign, there is a lack of pathos at the end of the book. Then, one page later, printed in a font different from the narrator's and from the characters' stories, there are two very short newspaper reports: the first briefly describing Selassie's last months and the other one – his death of natural causes. And that is all. No comment, no reflection, no analysis. Just emptiness.

Every time I finish reading *The Emperor*, I cannot help thinking that it is Kapuściński's best book. The utterly precise structure of the book undoubtedly contributes to this opinion. Also, the well constructed and well polished conflict of two idioms (and two worlds), which are very different from each other and compete against each other, but at the same time complete each other. Furthermore, the narrator's persona which keeps all the characters, information and book's structure in a tight tyrannical grip not unlike Selassie's many decades of control over Ethiopia. However, the crucial factor in forming the book's masterpiece status is that it is a cruelly acute, profound and exhaustive study of power, corruption and human folly.

Part Three
TRAUMA

I. Unfathomable *Imperium*

The idea of writing a book about Russia/Soviet Union must have gnawed at Kapuściński for many years. In *Imperium*, Kapuściński, a true communist believer, a person who officially gave up his Communist Party membership only in 1984 but never revised his socialist politics, describes the confrontation of his imagination and expectations of the empire against reality. His first and quite shocking contact with the Soviet Union happened early in his life, during the 1939 Soviet invasion of Poland's eastern regions (and Kapuściński's hometown Pińsk, among others). Ever since then, the Soviet Union had been an important presence and constituted a problematic entity against which his beliefs and convictions were measured. After World War II, Kapuściński traveled to Pińsk in 1979, having just finished *The Soccer War* (1978).[87] *The Soccer War,* a volume, which described the end of Portuguese power in Angola among other things and related the author's many adventures on the African and Latin American continents, differed significantly from his previous books. *The Soccer War* was Kapuściński's first attempt at structuring a reportage collection as an account of his own travel experiences. This form of a reportage 'memoir' he later mastered in *Imperium*.[88] Until *Imperium*, his dispatches from Africa, Latin America and the Middle East, and especially his profiles of tyrants, were laced with the subversive implications unmistakably deciphered by his readers, back then the enslaved inhabitants of the Polish People's Republic. In *Imperium* there needed not to be any twisted and subtle allusions to political systems, as the book was published in 1993 in Polish, and even later in English. The communist system had already collapsed; there was no censorship to deal with, no complicated system of Party relationships to be accounted for.

Kapuściński's first trip outside of Europe happened a bit unexpectedly; he was sent on an assignment to India (for a more detailed explanation see Part I – Introduction). After the journey to India, his newly discovered passion for travelling pushed Kapuściński to work outside Poland and Europe for the rest of his life in search of the speeding up of the historical processes. Kapuściński visited numerous remote regions and parts of Russia and the Soviet Union, not just the two, present and former, capitals. Yet, the trip turned out to be something very different to what had been originally designed. In *Imperium*, or

---

87 Beata Nowacka, Zygmunt Ziątek, *Ryszard Kapuściński: Biografia pisarza*, Kraków: Wydawnictwo Znak, 2008, p. 187.
88 Ryszard Kapuściński, *Imperium*, trans. Klara Glowczewska, New York: Alfred A Knopf, 1994. (all quotations in the text are from this edition). First Polish edition: Warszawa: Czytelnik, 1993.

more precisely while Kapuściński wrote it, he was almost 20 years older than he was while writing *The Emperor*. This, among other things, contributed to *Imperium* being unlike his previous works. He tried to recapitulate on his lifelong encounters with Russia, but found impossible to frame Russia within any precise confining categories, as he was both frightened by and fascinated by it. The topic was both close and uncomfortable for Kapuściński and, therefore, often emotional. In the 'Russian book,' he continued to use certain proven methods, such as adapting the point of view of a seemingly gullible and trusting wanderer, but employed other diverse methods to set the book apart from his 'African' and 'South American' books: in *Imperium*, unlike in any other books, the narration is very slow, its long sentences parallel the vast spaces of Russia. The unhurried stories and the lack of rigid structure of the book also mirror the crumbling of the former empire.

1. Attempt at autobiography

Imperium could be interpreted as an attempt at writing an autobiography, formed against the colossal and threatening Other. Kapuściński's Russian travels are flanked by the place of his origin, Pińsk. We encounter Pińsk on the first pages of the book, when the narrator together with his family, after having gone through the traumatic experiences of September 1939, leaves the town and heads toward the West. In the last chapter of the main part of the book, where he writes about the final stage of his Russian journey, which coincides with the final stage of existence of the Soviet Union, that is 1991, he returns to Pińsk. He enters the town from the East, as if – after having circled the entire globe – he was now coming back home. He ends the main text of *Imperium* with a short sentence (a rarity in the book, as most of the sentences are lengthy): "I had returned to my childhood home." It is, of course, a conscious procedure, meant to bring out the symbolic aspect of his travels. In reality, he had visited Pińsk in 1979, but he does not mention that visit in the book. The opening chapter of *Imperium*, which contains the description of the Soviet invasion of 1939, the terror and fear, the process of uprooting and leaving his home is one of the cruelest in Kapuściński's prose. It is very telling than that in his books he chooses situations that frighten other people, such as ethnic wars, the dissolution of nations, conflicts between hostile cultures. Moreover, most of his books are based on depicting his participation in violent wars, coups and bloody revolutions, on his surviving in the most unforgiving climates, in the sub-arctic circle, in the jungle and in the desert, his constantly getting in the harm's way and dodging death almost every step of the way. Yet none of those experiences can match the childhood trauma and the mark it left on the author's consciousness. It could be argued that closing the book with a return to his hometown is an attempt at restoring a symbolic end of his journey understood as a personal re-discovery of Russia and Pińsk through a mode of travel writing: the assumption is that after having returned home he can finally have normalcy and order. He no longer has to see Russia as a threat and a cause of childhood trauma, so the scary monster can be relinquished to the realm of childhood nightmares. Such is the postulation and hope for resolution of the trauma.

But no resolution happens.

Furthermore, the presence of a childhood trauma does not just serve a simple role of a source of childhood nightmares and fear of Russia. In fact, it is one of the essential elements of the book's structure.

II. Trauma and its consequences

> In its most general definition, trauma describes an overwhelming experience of sudden, or catastrophic events, in which the response to the event occurs in the often delayed, and uncontrolled repetitive occurrence of hallucinations and other intrusive phenomena,

explains Cathy Caruth while discussing Sigmund Freud's *Moses and Monotheism*.[89] Since Freud's times, an opinion that a significant childhood trauma is formative to the development of the ego, however controversial and far from grasping the complexities of the ego formation, has played a significant role in psychology. The constitution of the ego is often described as being formed in the process of dealing with traumatic experiences of pain and pleasure, and it is termed "the bitter practical experience" by Freud.[90] Freud's explanation is by no means the defining one. Caruth, for instance, interprets trauma as an abrupt event paving the way to one's freedom or as a form of memory frozen at a specific point in time. Moreover, without trauma, there is no possibility of history, claims Caruth: "Centering his story in the nature of the leaving, and returning, constituted by trauma, Freud resituates the very possibility of history in the nature of a traumatic departure" (184). For the Hebrews to become the Jews, according to Freud, it took a traumatic departure from Egypt. For Kapuściński to become the world famous reporter and writer it took a traumatic departure from Pińsk. A freeing departure. It gave Kapuściński a certain freedom, freedom to bring forth his voice to the world. The departure also enabled the relational aspect of his story, similarly to Freud's understanding of the history of the Jews – a universal prerequisite for relational history to happen. For history, like trauma, does not just belong or happen to one individual, history is "precisely the way we are implicated in each other's traumas" (189).

Steven Reisner in his discussion of psychic trauma sees it as a "an intersect of pain and truth." More specifically,

> [we] relegate the pain to certain privileged positions within our cultural narrative: most typically to the distant past of early childhood. Thus we draw on the authority of the past and the authority of pain and ourselves as the authors of that authority. And we draw on one more superseding authority: the authority of the story, what Freud called 'our mythology': the psychoanalytic theory we adhere to.[91]

---

89 Cathy Caruth, "Unclaimed Experience: Trauma and the Possibility of History," *Yale French Studies* 79 (1991): 181-92.

90 Sigmund Freud, *The Interpretations of Dreams*, translated by Joyce Crick, with an introduction and notes by Ritchie Robertson, Oxford: Oxford University Press, 1999, p. 446.

91 Steven Reisner, "Psychic Trauma and the Seductions of a Painful Past," *Studies in Gender and Sexuality* 4:3 (2003): 263-286.

Today's psychoanalysis is said to often rely on three authorities: the authority of the past, of pain and of theory. The authority of the past rests on the premise that early years of life border on its nonverbal phase and thus are close to unmodified truth. By beginning the book with a traumatic story from his childhood, Kapuściński minimizes the importance of references and facts but stresses the aspect of childhood impressions and emotions, which he presents as genuine. Even though the story, he signals, is going to be distorted and filtered through the traumatic repression, the frozen memory of a trauma preserves the impressions of the events in its 'true' form.

"The authority of theory is an attempt to aligning the analyst's therapeutic ego with a greater, more authoritative ego—the theoretical ego—presumably freed from the distortions of any individual ego process."[92] The authority of theory is a necessary one in the process of therapy: a therapist has to rely on a higher authority in order to protect the patient from any deformation the patient's or the therapist's egos might engage in. The opening chapter of *Imperium* is a brief, one-sided, abruptly ending story of a child traumatized by the Soviet invasion, while the rest of the book strives to show a multilayered and diverse picture of Russia. It could be said then that after telling the story of his early years, in the rest of *Imperium's* narrative Kapuściński aligns his position with a higher authority. It is the authority of wide knowledge, of numerous facts, multiaspectual depictions of Russia, in other words, of aspiring to objectivity. In numerous interviews and books, Kapuściński makes clear that in his opinion the strength of reportage lays in its inherent subjectivity.[93] As if to counter his own opinions, his descriptions of Russia aspire to 'objectivity': his encounters with the country are half a century long, he visits almost all the former Soviet Republics, describes places as different as Moscow, Vorkuta, Kiev, Petersburg, Chelabinsk, Dushanbe, Buchara, Drohobych, he presents numerous minorities, geographical regions, industrial enterprises, natural wonders, includes various quotes, fragments of books, articles, dialogs, conversations, opinions of his interlocutors, relations of his travels, descriptions of traditions, rituals, theatre plays, legends, political events. Consequently, the books is construed of two dissimilar parts: the initial chapter with the description of the childhood trauma which simultaneously possesses an evidently subjective character and an inherent 'truth' preserved by trauma, and the rest of the book with endless, multilayered, diverse descriptions of countless aspects of Russian life. The two opposite stances in *Imperium* are on one hand, striving for objectivity, and on the other, a certain resignation to subjectivity, highlighted by trauma.

---

92 Ibid, p. 276.
93 See for example: Witold Bereś, Krzysztof Burnetko, *Kapuściński: nie ogarniam świata*, Warszawa: Świat książki, 2007; or Ryszard Kapuściński, *Dałem głos ubogim: rozmowy z młodzieżą*, Kraków: Wydawnictwo Znak, 2008.

Even though Kapuściński clearly is the author of the entire book, it could be argued that he relegates the authorship of the second part of the book to presenting an objective view of Russia. This relegation, even though it pertains to the second part of the book, that is to his encounters with Russia as an adult, is, in my opinion, a consequence of the early childhood trauma. Trauma's consequences defined in this situation as an enforced passivity directed at the authorship of one's experience, can be tracked on the pages of the book, and even more widely, in Kapuściński's life, in the form of a certain conformity or even submissiveness in the face of power. The author's personality, recently portrayed in the controversial biography written by Artur Domosławski, was a curious mixture of incredible bravery and disturbing spinelessness. Kapuściński, along with decades of astonishing and daring acts such as traveling to the most Godforsaken places in the world and voluntarily putting himself in the harm's way in order to "give voice to those who did not have a voice,"[94] (as he himself, somewhat presumptuously said) was also known to majorly re-write and re-create many events of his life in order to please those in power.[95] It is rather impossible to resolve whether such servile behavior was a consequence of the significant trauma undergone by Kapuściński in childhood or simply an unpleasant feature of his personality, however, the traces of it are visible his texts, and most prominently in *Imperium*. L. L. Langer in his study of Holocaust testimonies has created a definition of 'humiliating memory': "Humiliating memory recalls an utter distress that shatters all molds designed to contain a unified and irreproachable image of the self."[96] In *Imperium* the destruction of the 'molds' is most clearly visible in the attempt to build an 'objective' and not the author's own picture of Russia.

---

94 Ryszard Kapuściński's *Dałem głos ubogim: rozmowy z młodzieżą* is a book of Kapuściński's conversations with students and youth published postmortem in 2008.

95 It can even be stated that expressions such as "give voice to those who did not have one" sound presumptuous as if Kapuściński saw himself a modern version Christ; they also direct our attention to the fact that his ethics have been close to the utopian communism, at least rhetorically.

96 L. L. Langer, *Holocaust Testimonies: The Ruins of Memory*, New Haven, CT: Yale University Press, 1999, p. 77.

III. Structure

Kapuściński's impressions from his trip to the Russian Federation at the beginning of the 1990s were invariability, inability, the society unprepared to modify its life according to new conditions and idly waiting to have its lives structured or returned back to the strict rules, secret police and terror. The author does not describe the revolutionary changes, the sped-up social processes, the rapid ending to historical formations – such as those he presented in *The Emperor*, *Shah of Shah* or in *Another Day of Life*. On the one hand, he definitely recognizes the unmistakable symptoms of a closing stage of a colonial power, which he had witnessed many times before, only on different continents. The symptoms were clearly present in the borderland republics in Central Asia and the Caucasus, and included the departure of the white (that is of course, Russian) colonizers, the disintegration of the colonizers' forms of government, roaming troops, and the reluctance to communicate in the language of the colonizers.

The Soviet Union was an ethnically and culturally diverse formation, supported in many of its parts by the constantly threatening presence of the Red Army troops. Therefore, in 1991, the Soviet colossus was falling down unevenly, at different paces in various parts of the country, and in some parts the disintegration was not happening at all. The change was not as abrupt and violent as the crumbling of colonial powers in Africa. Kapuściński was confused by what seemed to him like the lack of a clear historical change and a visible societal shift of which he was so keen and for which he had developed cognitive tools throughout the years of travelling. Faced with an unclear and diversified transformation Kapuściński often resorts to stereotypes, patronizing tone and oversimplifications:

> Description of demolishing of the Temple of Christ the Savior in Moscow:
>
> Stalin orders the largest sacral object in Moscow to be razed. Let us for a moment give free to our imagination. It is 1931. Let us imagine that Mussolini, who at that time rules Italy, orders the Basilica of St. Peter in Rome to be razed. Let us imagine that Paul Doumer, who is at that time president of France, orders the Cathedral of Notre-Dame in Paris to be razed. Let us imagine that Poland's Marshall Jozef Pilsudski orders that Jasnogorski Monastery in Czestochowa to be razed.
> Can we imagine such a thing?
> No.
>
> (The Temple and The Palace, 99)

According to Kapuściński, in enlightened Europe such horrible events as razing the main temple of a nation are impossible, and they can happen only in backwards, tyrant-ruled Russia. What Kapuściński curiously fails to remember is that only 8 years after the demolishing of the Temple of Christ the Savior in Moscow, Nazi Germany invades Poland and no temples or anything else remains sacred.

About the Caucasus and the mindset of its inhabitants:

> The second thing that is immediately noticeable is the immemoriality of prevailing judgments, the tyranny of stereotypes. Here everything was fixed, determined, defined in times that have receded into the obscure mists of history. No one is really able to explain why Armenians and Azerbaijanis hate each other. They hate each other and that's that! Everyone knows this; everyone imbibed this with his mother's milk. This immutability of judgments was fostered by mutual isolation (mountains!) and by the fact that the entire region of the Caucasus was squeezed in between very backwards countries—Iran, Russia and Turkey. Contact with the liberal and democratic thinking of the West was impossible, and existing neighbors did not provide constructive examples; there wasn't anyone to learn from.

(Man on an Asphalt Mountain, 126)

Putting aside such obvious fact that mountains do not have to create an isolating barrier (the highlanders from Slovakia and Poland do not seem to be isolated from each other by the Tatra mountains), saying that Iran, Russia and Turkey are "backwards" is nothing short of offensive. The worst thing, however, in this short fragment is Kapuściński's assumption that people of Armenia and Azerbaijan are not capable of creating and developing their own critical and independent thinking and the only way for them to develop such skills and to respect their neighbor is to learn from the West. Which comes as a surprise after reading *Imperium's* chapter-long praises of the age-old Caucasus countries, their cultures, architecture, religion and art.

About a miners' strike in Vorkuta:

> I can see that these poor, frozen people, people who often do not see the light of day for weeks at a time, are being fooled by this man who yesterday returned from Moscow, are being fooled and hoaxed. I can see it, but there is nothing I can do about it; I cannot stand up and cry: People, don't believe him! I cannot, if only so as not do deprive them of that shred of comfort that they derive from the thought that Vargashovska will be exporting coal to England and America.

(Vorkuta, To Freeze in Fire, 162)

Again, only Kapuściński is able to see that the miners are being fooled by the director of the mine, not one of them possesses the capability of thinking on his own.

Passages like these are present throughout the book; through them it becomes apparent that Kapuściński is struggling with the topic. He might be, on a bigger scale, making amends with the West and on a smaller, more personal scale, trying to come to terms with his erstwhile loyal support for the Soviet-type of socialism and his conflict with post-1989 reality. To his defense, it should be stated that he was not isolated in looking at Russia through such biased lens. Richard Pipes as late as 1997 says "A modified Brezhnev Doctrine is still in force... Decolonization has been quite halfhearted."[97]

When Kapuściński cannot find the abrupt and unstable, to which he is accustomed, he often invokes a popular, however clichéd opinion that Russia is too big and too mysterious to be described. As if overwhelmed by the size and incomprehensibility of Russia and his inability to create a well rounded narrative, in a manner more modest than usual, he shares with the reader his knowledge presented in micro-stories, miniature narratives, trivial pictures. The shift to concentrate on daily aspects of life, the mundane and everyday and randomly met people disappointed many readers, who expected an extensive work similar to *The Emperor* or *Another Day of Life* – all-embracing syntheses and broad descriptions of turning points in contemporary history. Adam Hochschild says,

> The analogy between the USSR and the Western colonial powers has been made before, but seldom, I suspect, by someone with Kapuściński's experience of both systems. I only wish he had explored it at more length and more systematically. Being a miniaturist serves him somewhat less well here.[98]

Robert Levold, on the other hand, expresses his partial disappointment about *Imperium* that it is "not a set of essays, and even less a detailed assessment of the reality he encounters."[99] The critical remarks by American reviewers attest to their, if not complete, then definitely partial, readerly sense of insufficiency in *Imperium*.[100]

---

97   Richard Pipes, "Is Russia Still an Enemy?," *Foreign Affairs* 76:5 (Sept-Oct 1997): 73.
98   Adam Hochschild, "Magic Journalism," *New York Review of Books* 41:18 (Nov. 1994).
99   Robert Legvold, Review of *Imperium*, *Foreign Affairs* 73: 6 (1994): 178.
100 The reviewers expressed their disappointment not only in the author's method and the structure of the book; the translation of *Imperium* was criticized as well. Adam Hochschild in the afore-mentioned book's review words it perfectly: "Unfortunately the copy-editing of the English translation of *Imperium* is not on a par with Kapuściński's writing. One can forgive the occasional incorrect usage ("conveyances" where "convoys" is called for) but not the strange transliteration of Russian names long familiar to English-speaking readers in other spellings. We read, for example, about "Cvietayeva" and "Char'kov" rather than Tsvetayeva and Kharkov. Worse is the mangling of the English-language titles of books Kapuściński refers to. Roy Medvedev's classic account of the Stalin years appeared in the US not as "Under the Judgment of History" but as *Let History Judge*. In passing from Russian to Polish to English, some things have gotten even more garbled. Kapuściński several times quotes Eugenia Ginzburg's great memoir of the *gulag*, which is entitled in Russian *Krutoi Marshrut*. *Krutoi* can mean either

2. Structure

By focusing not on change, but on the unchanging elements, not on what was new and different, but on what was old and repeated, the author turns to the deeply hidden strength of the imperial Russian stance and in a way chooses essence over existence. It can be argued that the permanence of a system might be most visible when seen in accidentally selected places, moments and circumstances, instead of carefully chosen, often staged-out situations. At the same time, it might as well be something to be expected in a country where the population was subjected to many decades of brain-washing. Of course, there are no *truly* random cases in *Imperium*; all those accidental situations are heavy on their symbolism, such 10-year old Tanya from Yakutsk who knows 'real' freezing temperatures and knows how to jump over mud puddles in spring; the sturdy old babushka who answers "Dishim!" to the author asking her how she is doing; the miners in Vorkuta who try to run a meeting aimed at defying the mine's directors, but none of the directors is present to tell the workers how to run such a meeting, so the miners go home having achieved nothing; professor Grekov in Novgorod, who for 25 years has been trying to restore several-hundred-years old church frescoes broken into hundreds of little pieces during the Nazi bombardments of the city. Such 'little pictures' reveal a human element of life in the Soviet Union, an element which for a long time was blocked from the official reports: people resigning to their fate, fearing strangers, feeling lost and helpless

---

"steep" or "severe," "drastic," etc. *Marshrut* comes from the French *marche* and *route*. Hence a literal translation of the phrase might be something like "Arduous Road." But the book's name appears here, bizarrely, as "The Steep Wall," matching neither the Russian meaning nor the title of the American edition, *Journey into the Whirlwind* (Harcourt Brace Jovanovich, 1967). A writer of Kapuściński's stature deserves more care from his publisher than this." I also would like to mention one more problem that Adam Hochshild might have missed: the translation of the two lines of Adam Mickiewicz's "Reduta Ordona – Opowiadania adiutanta" on page 88 of the English translation is most likely Glowczewska's own, as it does not resemble any of the poem's translations I have read: "The Czar is surprised—the inhabitants of Petersburg tremble with fear, / The Czar is angry—his courtiers die of fear; armies are marching, whose God and faith / is the Czar. The Czar is angry: let us die, we will cheer up the Czar!"; there is no footnote, no reference explaining where the quote came from or who the author of these lines was; the lines are incorporated in the text and they are not set apart from it. The Polish original of the poem inserted seamlessly into Kapuściński's text is as follows: "Car dziwi się - ze strachu mrą Petersburczany, / Car gniewa się – ze strachu mrą jego dworzany; / Ale sypią się wojska, których Bóg i wiara / Jest Car. – Car gniewny: umrzem, rozweselim Cara!" While it is easy for a Polish reader to recognize Mickiewicz's name and lines of the poem, the English-speaking reader might simply be confused by them and lack of any reference.

when facing the waywardness of authority, and the impossibility of having an authentic cultural tradition (as everything was orchestrated by higher authorities). But those more human elements, those mini-stories, trivial everyday events are not enough to give the book a clearly defined identity; not enough to impose limits encompassing the huge amounts of material Kapuściński collects during the course of his travels to the Soviet Union and Russia. As a result, *Imperium*, as opposed to *The Emperor*, is not rigidly and precisely structured. Many stories are loosely tied to each other, sometimes not even resulting from each other. The end of *Imperium* brings no summation to the problems presented in the stories as the narrative does not end in a neat and all-embracing conclusion. The whole narrative simply fades away, disappears in the horizon, leaving the reader with all the problems described and without any resolutions.

The opening chapter of the book focuses on a childhood recollection of the Red Army troops taking over Pińsk. We read descriptions of train cars full of Polish wrong-thinkers selected for 'zsyłka' to Siberia; the drunken Soviet soldiers bombarding the town's church tower; and hungry boys licking the insides of empty tin candy cans and playing on a broken merry-go-round in freezing weather. These pictures are not long, full of details and names; on the contrary, they are merely sketches, but their cruel simplicity is heartrending.

I have said that Kapuściński, the reporter and narrating voice/narrator, is the main character of the books written by Kapuściński, the author. Therefore, the fact the author himself relates the events of "Pińsk," the opening chapter of *Imperium*, is not different from his other works. The element that constitutes the crucial difference, however, is that in all other books the main character is an adult – someone who consciously *chooses* to be where he is – scared, hungry, on the verge of death, pleading his way out of some terrifying situation. In *Imperium* we see him in similar circumstances, but this is an ordeal of a *child*, a helpless, starving and frightened child. Understandably then, the tone of the first chapter is very intimate, much more private than in any other accounts of his travels. He admits to the fact that his vision of Russia was skewed from the very beginning, from the very first encounter, as it was shaped by the shock caused by the invading Soviet troops. *Imperium* then, can be read as a narration of personal therapy, as if in the author's perception for the rest of his life Russia and everyone else exerting power remained the monster of childhood dreams entirely beyond control and comprehension but such that had to be pleased and appeased. In another words, the therapy is not entirely successful.

For Kapuściński, Russia could not be described, could not be limited by any borders (even literary) or metaphors, but it could be used to try to restore one's own personal order. Up until *Imperium*, Kapuściński made the reader accustomed to fascinating analogies and all-embracing metaphors. However, in this book, he does not create an all-encompassing metaphor or an acute study of power. *Imperium*, with a much more personal character than his other books, can then be treated as an attempt to come to terms with the presence of the Russian Other.

Another aspect of *Imperium*, which attests to its personal character, is the focus only on Russia, both imperial and post-Soviet. The presence of the Soviet Union is scarce, except for the first chapter containing the accounts of the 1939 invasion and the short account of Kapuściński's travels in the late 1950s and 60s. In addition, the vivacity of the small cultures, which were able to survive the Soviet (and earlier Russian) occupation, is emphasized throughout the entire book. It is an extremely subjective way of presenting this vast and diverse country, a way that fits the already established assumption. It is, I might venture to say, a 'Polish' way of seeing Russia. In reality, Kapuściński visited the Soviet Union in 1957 during the Festival of the World Students and Youth (that is when he met the young oppositionists from African countries, who later became the leaders of newly independent African states and from whom Kapuściński got the enthusiasm for their cause).[101] That event is not even mentioned in the descriptions of his Russian travels in mid-20th century. Instead, according to the book, after September 1939, the next time the author encountered the Russian Other was on his way from China to Poland on the Trans-Siberian train, in 1958. The train trip lasted two weeks and inscribed itself ideally into the typical Polish Romantic discourse of an arduous 'zsyłka.' In the description of the train trip the only difference between Kapuściński and 'zesłańcy' seemed to be that the author was travelling west, instead of east.

3. Russia as Poland's big Other

Maxim Waldstein, the author of an article which put *Imperium* under a close scrutiny suggests that the book inscribes itself into the process of re-creating the Central European identity shaken and weakened by centuries of Russian occupation, manipulation and exploitation.[102] Waldstein claims that in the book, the subject of the orientalizing gaze is a formerly colonized Pole and its object is the former empire, which is quite a different understanding of an orientalizing gaze to Edward Said's definition in *Orientalism*. According to Waldstein, *Imperium* is another strong critique of totalitarianism and imperialism that Kapuściński

---

101 *Ryszard Kapuściński: Biografia…*, p. 357.
102 Maxim K. Waldstein, "Observing *Imperium*: A Postcolonial Reading of Ryszard Kapuściński's Account of Soviet and Post-Soviet Russia," *Social Identities* 8: 3 (2002): 481-499.

penned, and in that sense it belongs to the Kapuściński-esque type of creative nonfiction. At the same time, the author of the article says that the most important characteristic distinguishing the book from other nonfiction works is that *Imperium* is an Orientalist text aimed at the visualization of the inferior and dangerous Other. It is a reckoning with the empire deeply engrained in Kapuściński's consciousness, and is a certain kind of therapy, which helps him free himself from the empire's oppressive presence. The process, as maintained by Waldstein, can also be seen as a more general process of Eastern European countries liberating themselves from centuries of the Russian/Soviet domination. While some of Waldstein's statements are definitely valuable, I disagree with the statement that Kapuściński has to free himself from Russia in order to *form* his identity. While Russia, or rather the Soviet Union, played an important role in his identity forming process, Kapuściński's identity was not formed solely around Russia. Russia was only one of the elements, which caused his trauma, Nazi Germany was another element. His identity was of course built around several factors, where the trauma of war, his national and ideological identity and the need for engagement were, arguably, the most important. It is more appropriate to say that the childhood trauma caused by the invasion of the Red Army and then the escape from the Soviet occupied Polesie to Nazi occupied Poland were a factor, which was actually *prohibiting* Kapuściński from achieving some kind of state of freedom and normalcy. Therefore, Waldstein's accusations of Kapuściński throwing an orientalizing gaze at the fearsome and oppressive Other have some value, but do not take into account all the complexities of the writer's identity formation process.

4. Russia's inhuman size

> The border is stress—fear, even (significantly more rarely: liberation). The concept of the border can include a kind of finality; the door can slam shut behind of forever: such is the border between life and death. The gods know about such anxieties, and that is why they try to win adherents by promising people that as a reward they will enter the divine kingdom—which will have no borders. The paradise of the Christian God, the paradise of Yahweh and Allah, all have no borders. Buddhists know that the state of nirvana is the state of blissful happiness without limits. In short, that which is most desired, awaited, and longed for by everyone is precisely this unconditional, total, absolute—boundlessness (21).

The author of *Imperium* is well acquainted with the human fear of anything limitless and the need of setting all kinds of borders. Kapuściński juxtaposes the fear with the notion of borderlessness, that is a divine, non-human aspect. He even develops the concept further and sees the annihilation of limits as a characteristic of gods and god-like creations – a synonym of freedom. As if to contradict his ponderings, Russia, because of its enormous, almost brutal size, becomes nearly borderless. Never in its history has the 'nonexistence' of Russia's borders translated into lack of restrictions and liberty, support of individualism and adventurous attitude according to Kapuściński; on the contrary, for millions of enslaved people the country had been a vast prison, out of which there was no chance of escaping.

In the book, even nature corroborates the view of Russia's oppressive vastness and enormousness. A lake in Russia has to be the deepest in the world, the climate – the coldest on Earth, the taiga – impassable, the tundra – impenetrable. The landscape visibly overpowers and dominates the narrative during the author's trip on the Trans-Siberian train. The Siberian nature is so powerful that it intervenes with the book's narrative – the notes from the trip are short, weary, written with clear difficulty. Hence comes the conclusion that Russia is too immense to be comprehended as a whole; instead, a fragmentary approach is necessary to even approach it.

As mentioned above, Hochschild claims that Kapuściński's 'miniaturist' approach usually serves him well, but in his descriptions of Russia it can be seen as a hindrance. But the fragmentary approach is the author's conscious creation and, in some way, a continuation from other books. In *Imperium*, Russia has a god-like size and is incomprehensible in its entirety; thus it has to be dealt with in a fractional way. Encountering Russia, as the opening chapter of the book proves, is traumatic, therefore like many traumas it is bearable only when handled in metonymical parts. This, in turn, does not mean that knowledge of Russia's metonymical parts can lead to knowing the entirety of it.

The fragmentary approach is visible not just in the author's relation with Russia. In his descriptions of Russia, even its inhabitants and authorities have to divide it, fragment it, to make it graspable and controllable. Most importantly, it is information that has to be broken into pieces. Kapuściński writes that the Soviet system guarded information much more carefully than the weapons of mass destruction. Brezhnev, when asked what could be written about the 1968 Soviet invasion of Czechoslovakia, told the journalists that they could write everything, but only in one copy, which was to be sent directly to him (214). Kapuściński verges on sarcasm when he sums up the paranoid Soviet economy with a scornful concept: Why is it impossible to buy a hoe in Smolensk? Because the entire metallurgy industry is making barbed wire for the borders and gulags, which are countless and immeasurable, like Russia itself.

5. Doting on minorities

The entire chapter titled "The South '67" contains descriptions of the author's travels to the outskirts of the Soviet Union in the late 1960's. In it, Kapuściński emphatically contrasts the beautiful, lively and colorful small countries (then: Soviet Republics) with grey, shabby and solemn Russia proper; countries with histories going back thousands of years: Armenia, Georgia, Azerbaijan, Turkmenia, Tajikistan, Kyrgyzstan and Uzbekistan. Kapuściński makes his affection for the colonized minorities no secret and explicitly expresses his tenderness. In his description of Yerevan he writes:

> I am returning to the hotel. It is an early autumn evening, warm, mild. Crowds of strolling people. There is a kind of friendliness to these streets, to this town. In one of the back alleys, in the depths of darkness, live embers are glowing. A small boy is sitting by an iron stove. He is broiling shish kebabs. His large black eye stare at the fire. A fascinated, almost unconscious gaze, as if beyond place, beyond time (119).

He seems to cherish the prospect that Russia, having lost its outer colonies, faces the danger of being divided by the Bashkirs, Yakuts and other minorities. He dotes on the oppressed minorities and small nations, because they,

> [...] despite the stiff, rigorous corset of Soviet power, the local, small, yet very ancient, nations has succeeded in preserving something of their tradition, of their history, of their, albeit, concealed pride and dignity. I discovered there, spread out in the sun, an Oriental carpet, which in many places still retained its age-old colors and the eye-catching variety of its original designs (38).

He shows respect for the small nations for enormous efforts to retain their identity during centuries of oppression. This is not so say that with all this affection he becomes blind to the problems and difficulties faced by these nations, out of which extreme nationalism is the most dangerous one. The Armenians' virulent hatred of the Azerbaijanis causes his eventual detachment from people taken hold by the folly of extreme nationalism. Kapuściński's view of a small nation's nationalism is in line with Isiah Berlin's concept of the bent twig.[103]

Not surprisingly, in Kapuściński's opinion the crucial element of retaining identity of the colonized minorities is language. In the part on Tajikistan of "The South '67" chapter, Kapuściński writes down an anecdote about a young Tajik who came back to his village from the war, spoke only Russian and claimed he forgot how to speak Tajik (72). The villagers gathered in front of his house to see what a Tajik who had forgotten his language looked like. The entire village stood in front of his house, and all of a sudden the villagers started laughing at someone who did not want to speak their own language, they laughed and

---

103 Isiah Berlin, "The Bent Twig: A Note on Nationalism," *Foreign Affairs* 51 (Oct 1972): 11-30.

laughed... Finally, the young Tajik shouted: 'Enough!' (in Tajik) and started laughing himself. "That day on which the young Tajik remembered his native tongue, a sheep was slaughtered in the village, and everyone feasted all night," which not surprisingly sounds like a fairy tale ending.

The author has a similar attitude toward the importance of preserving the native language in Ukraine. In the chapter "Pomona of the Little Town of Drohobych," dedicated in its entirety to Ukraine, he writes about the struggle of Ukrainians to preserve their language. Through the example of a local poet, Ivan Drach, who had to abandon writing poetry and took up working in the community as "one must put poetry aside, and save the Ukraine, save its culture," shows the previously oppressed nations' belief in the significance of protecting their national legacy (279). Kapuściński quotes Drach who says that at the beginning of the 1990's "Russification is so advanced that in a few years' time there will be no one left who can read new Ukrainian literature. Besides, one must first restore the existing literature to its reader." Kapuściński finds that the concern for national legacy and identity by nations, which had been colonized by Russia, is the same regardless of their geography.

6. "Naïve" wanderer

Throughout the book, Kapuściński consciously and consistently maintains his image as a naïve and gullible traveler. He often gets in trouble, since he has to experience everything himself and consciously puts himself in a position of a bit too trusting, a bit too vapid victim of circumstance. He goes as far as the eye can see and is almost annoying in this simplicity and naïveté. He usually is on the receiving end of things, rarely shows his agency. The author never talks about his dealings with authorities – as we now know, he had made deals with communist authorities in Poland, and we can assume that in the visited countries he too had some kind of arrangements with the local authorities.[104] There have been many publications in Poland and abroad describing Kapuściński's conscious co-operation with the Polish Secret Police – Służba Bezpieczeństwa, most of which had taken place in the second half of the 1960's and the beginning of the 1970's.[105] According to many authors of his biographies, most importantly Artur Domosławski, Kapuściński chose to not ignore the offers from the Secret Police. In order to be allowed to freely travel around the world, he played a complicated game with the authorities to simultaneously keep his official credentials as a Polish journalist and appease the recruiting Służba Bezpieczeństwa officers.

---

104 Artur Domosławski, *Kapuściński: Non-fiction*, Warszawa: Świat książki, 2010.
105 See *Newsweek* (2007): No 11, p. 111 & No 21, p. 36.

The persona he uses in his books is of course a conscious creation, and his method of creating it is deceptively simple. To a certain extent, the fact that he presents himself as a naïve and humble wanderer is an opposition to Western image-driven media and the aggressive commercialization of mainstream journalism, and stemming from it – the indifference to many serious problems plaguing today's world. The meek and mellow attitude is also another way of aligning himself with the "subaltern," with the seemingly random simple people he meets and describes. Through the creation of his literary alter ego, he asserts the association with the Third World (simplicity), and opposes the First World (unnecessary complexity and commercialization).[106]

7. Narrator is no tyrant

Many of Kapuściński's books are written with the use of short, dynamic sentences, containing few adjectives. Information is rendered in a simple, straightforward way; there are many dialogs and brief news reports, making his texts dynamic and easily understandable. *Imperium* differs from the author's other books even in this aspect. In the 'Russian' book the sentences are long, drawn-out, lingering, reflecting the author's perception of Russia, for instance his journey on the train from Harbim to Moscow. As I have said before, Kapuściński aids himself with many long quotations, stretched references, extended descriptions borrowed from other writers, news agencies and textbooks, attempting to render Russia's picture as 'objective' as possible.

There are several elements constituting a connection between all the parts of the otherwise loosely tied narrative: the narrator and his childhood trauma, and as a result of it – his re-written life, the framing role ascribed to Pińsk and, of course, Russia. The structure, on which the narrative is built, is the constantly fluctuating relationship between these elements. The narrator makes repeated attempts at assuming authority over the text, but he never fully succeeds. *Imperium's* narrator is not oppressive in his presence nor can he assume an authority over the text, since the text of *Imperium* is not monolithic. The imprecise structure of *Imperium* and its narrative, loosely tied and consisting of many seemingly unrelated parts, prevent the narrator from becoming a tyrant within the text. I have previously noted that Russia's enormous size and its incomprehensibility force the author to assume a fragmentary approach to the topic. Such fragmentary, at times even disconnected, approach further undermines the narrator's authority. The narrator is not the one who rules over the text; in *Imperium* it is much more as if the topic, its size, its incomprehensibility and the chronology dictated

---

[106] It is arguable whether Kapuściński indeed sees entire Russia as a Third World country, however, it should be stated that in his descriptions of some parts of Russia (especially the borderlands) there are definite characteristics of a poor, developing country.

what happened in the narrative. Thus the narrator's language does not constitute any kind of distinct idiom within the narrative.

However, the narrator makes repeated attempts throughout the text at establishing his authority, for instance in the description of Moscow ("The Third Rome," 95), he repeatedly says "jak powiadam." The use of the frequentative archaic verb 'powiadać,' instead of the more common 'mówić,' 'stwierdzać,' or 'sądzić,' indicates an attempt of introducing a high style, or even the Biblical style (since this is where 'powiadać' is seen most often) and ascribing importance to the narrator's opinions.

Also in "Third Rome," when using an explanation why it is impossible to buy a hoe in Smolensk (because the entire Soviet metallurgy industry is busy making barbed wire to fence in the gulags) the narrator builds long, pompous, newspeak-type-of descriptions of Soviet reality, modeled on the communist party's functionaries' rants. The descriptions go on for pages, but the narrator – as if in the effort of reminding his readers that these describe a falsified reality – interjects them with short, sarcastic phrases, always separated from the text of a 'rant' with brackets.

Imperium has two endings. In the first, entitled "The Sequel Continues," the narrator in a bit incoherent and dull way reflects on the significance of the 1990's as the years marking the end of the Soviet system and leaves the reader with a mildly optimistic view of the future. He founds it on a cliché conviction of the West's never-ending willingness to help Russia based on West's fear and fascination of Russia. In the second ending, which in English, unlike in the Polish version, is simply inserted into the main text of "The Sequel," Kapuściński adds a short quotation from Leo Tolstoy's *War and Peace* – a description of Nikolai driving his troika through a vast, moon-lit winter landscape – conveying once again an atmosphere of uncertainty, overpowering nature and being at a loss. In the Polish version, in contrast, this quotation is set apart from the text on a separate page. In both versions, there is no definitive ending to the book; things are left hanging. Neither ending provides the reader with resolutions to any of the parts of the narrative. Adam Hochschild believes that the last sentence of the chapter preceding the final chapter ("Return to my Hometown") where the narrator states with relief "I had returned to my childhood home," actually concludes the book. He also says that the final chapter describing the situation in Russia in the 1990's was added at the request of the editor to bring the book up to date and that it does not serve the book well.[107] In my opinion, the presence of two different endings perfectly highlights the narrator's helplessness and failure to rule over the book's narrative.

---

107 Hochschild, "Magic Journalism…"

IV. (No) Resolution

The problem of *Imperium's* text preventing the narrator from assuming authority over itself is very telling. It is as if the main topic, Russia, was enough of a despotic power within the text, and the text could not carry any more tyranny. The author is aware of Russia's intimidating presence and constructs his narrator's image as a humbled man who starts to feel the burden of age. Furthermore, *Imperium's* narrator is a man who is not anymore keen on any type of tyranny, even his own over the book's narrative.

Hochschild also proposes that the childhood trauma caused by the Red Army invasion and by the Nazi occupation of Poland to which Kapuściński was a direct witness in his early years touched him in a special way: he developed an acute sense of the presence of tyranny, of totalitarianism.[108] While it might as well be true, it has to be stated directly that for many years Kapuściński's sense of tyranny was directed only at a certain type of tyranny – such that was not tied in any way to communism. His decades-long unrelenting faith in the ethics of the communist system was proverbial. It is still a matter of heated discussion whether he consciously turned a blind eye to the atrocities committed by the functionaries of the communist systems both in Poland and in the rest of the world or uncritically believed in the rightness of the system and through that justified all of its wrongdoings. Most of his reflections on poverty and exploitation either in the form or books or interviews and articles are done from the position of a true believer in communism and a harsh critic of the generally understood West. Such attitude sees its culmination in *The Emperor* written from a clearly pro-Soviet stance.

To his defense, it has to be said that Kapuściński's tendentious and approving attitude toward the world-wide efforts to introduce the "dictatorship of the proletariat" undertaken by the Soviet Union and its allies ended long before the Soviet Union fell in 1991. Admittedly, he gave up his Party membership only in 1984, but it was the time he spent with the striking workers of the Gdańsk Shipyard in August of 1980 and then General Jaruzelski's Martial Law imposed on December 13th 1981 that finally undermined his faith in communism. His books written after that are no longer as favorably inclined toward "the only true and right" ideology as his earlier works. As a result of all this, in *Imperium* Kapuściński re-invents his relationship with Russia and at the same time bids farewell to it. Before *Imperium*, his narratives are creations in which he is undoubtedly the only ruler. *Imperium* differs from his previous books because of the trauma, which stayed with him forever and the unfaltering and unrelenting

---

108 Hochschild, "Magic Journalism…"

topic that could not be controlled. Another reason is that together with the author's worldview changing there happens a noticeable shift in his method of writing. In other words, the transformation of his consciousness is followed by the process of differentiation of his writing and the search for a different formal method. The most significant transformation is a new concept of a narrator, which eventually bears fruit in the form of *Travels with Herodotus*.

Part Four
TALES

I. Reportage from the Self

Culled from several decades of his writing, *Lapidaria* by Ryszard Kapuściński differs significantly in form and poetics from his earlier works.[109] In it, Kapuściński turns inward and undertakes a journey of self-reflection. The texts gathered in *Lapidaria*, often as short as a few lines or a single page, include observations of the contemporary world, philosophical reflections on our civilization at the beginning of the third millennium, notes remembered from many decades of traveling, and, perhaps most interestingly, for my purposes, observations about his own writing process and experience as a journalist. *Lapidaria* is composed primarily of literary vignettes, often containing only a few sentences, and of quotations and references to works by other authors.

In *Lapidaria* the author employs a fragmentary aesthetics, which might be related to his understanding of the structure memory processes and their inescapable incompleteness. Kapuściński does not build all-embracing metaphors or look at the big picture; he concentrates on his impressions, feelings, perceptions. Such a fragmentary approach is also less limiting in a way, as there are no narrative or structural limitations. It could be said that *Lapidaria* is Kapuściński's preparation for writing *Travels with Herodotus* such that he attempts to free himself from the structural and ideological limitations he imposed on himself during decades of writing.

After having earned a reputation as an insightful reporter, coherent thinker, and outstanding writer, Kapuściński chooses to speak about himself more openly in *Lapidaria* than anywhere else by revealing his private opinions, and without calling upon his usual simple-minded heroes of the everyday struggle.[110] Although it should be noted that he does not do so completely openly, since he does not really speak about his engagement with the communist system or his unrelenting faith in the communist ideology. An inward journey, *Lapidaria* is a clear break from Kapuściński's typical narrative structure; almost everything in his daily life becomes material for reflection, including his interests, trivial problems, everyday occurrences, and sometimes simplistic truths about the society around him: "No one writes books anymore. Everyone wants to write a bestseller;" or "Videotapes force on people today not only a technique of seeing, but one of reading too: the reader wants to have the whole story in three minutes"

---

109 *Lapidaria* appeared as five separate volumes, published consecutively: *Lapidarium I* in1990, *Lapidarium II* in 1996, *Lapidarium III* in 1997, *Lapidarium IV* in 2000 and *Lapidarium V* in 2002. All the volumes were published by Czytelnik in Warsaw.

110 Compare with Chapter 2, Section III "Characters vs. Discourse," or Chapter 3, Section IV "Structure."

(217). Such examples illustrate an important tendency towards the aphoristic style in Kapuściński's writing.

Lapidaria is essentially reportage of the self, which reveals much about Kapuściński's famous methods of observing trivial, everyday events and participating in the lives of people he describes. Scattered randomly throughout the volumes of *Lapidaria* are confessions about Kapuściński's own writing techniques: "Usually I try to write short sentences, because they create tempo and movement. They are quick and give the prose clarity" (211); about his strategies for expanding the limits of language: "I need poetry, as a linguistic exercise; I cannot give up poetry. It demands a deep concentration on the language, and this results in good prose" (212); and even the place that his writing occupies in today's literary discourse:

> I see myself as a researcher of Otherness – of other cultures, different ways of thinking, different behaviors. I want to encounter strangeness – understood in its positive sense; strangeness which I like to come in contact with, in order to understand it. The question is always, how to describe present-day reality in a new and adequate way? Sometimes this kind of writing is called non-fiction writing. I would say that it's about non-fiction creative writing (211).

There is a trend of gradually internalizing the discourse throughout the book. Kapuściński slowly but surely goes from vivid descriptions of the landscapes he saw and the local traditions he witnessed during his many travels around the world to detailed observations of his own opinions, feelings, and memories. At the beginning of the book, the reader encounters whole stories, almost mini-reportages. Progressively, the narration of *Lapidaria* narrows down, even withdrawing entirely from crucial world affairs and politics, and turns into a careful, focused examination of the self. In this work Kapuściński takes an inward journey, which he makes as interesting as his previous travels around the world. The author's reflections on the fate of the world and contemplations on the state of contemporary man are often directly addressed to the reader or maybe to the author himself: "It is crucial that you maintain the ability to fully experience, that there exist things which are able to amaze you, cause a shock. It is crucial that you do not get infected with a horrible disease – indifference" (200).

In the Polish original: „Ważne jest, abyś zachował zdolność przeżywania, aby istniały rzeczy, które mogą cię zadziwić, wywołać wstrząs. Ważne jest, aby nie dotknęła cię straszna choroba – obojętność." Kapuściński employs the masculine second person form of the verb "zachować" (maintain, preserve) when addressing his audience. Admittedly, the masculine gender is often considered the default one in the Polish language; however, by simply switching the sentence to the plural number, the author could have avoided the heavily marked masculine gender. It can also be said that by using the masculine gender

Kapuściński almost systematically excludes women from his discourse; or, that many of his statements are really addressed to himself.

While reflecting and contemplating the current state of affairs, Kapuściński instructs his readers, and thus indirectly himself to always remain open to the world's wonders and most importantly, to empathize with all its creatures. As dreadfully sentimental and naïve as such statements sound, they are a testament to Kapuściński's insatiable ethnographic curiosity and openness to learning about other cultures.

II. Traveling with the Father of History

Travels with Herodotus was published in Polish in 2004 by The Publishing House Znak in Kraków as *Podróże z Herodotem*.[111] In accordance with a linear, chronological reading tradition, *Lapidaria* could be treated as a preface to *Travels*, Kapuściński's last and most reflexive book. *Travels with Herodotus* is an extensive report and a colorful tale from Kapuściński's inaugural journeys to foreign lands and the awakening of his reportorial sensitivity to otherness. In *Travels*, he crosses the borders of time and of space, with the narration happening simultaneously on several temporal and spatial planes. The accounts of his first several foreign reporting trips are interwoven with fragments from *The Histories* by Herodotus, which Kapuściński apparently had in tow throughout his entire professional life (it is difficult to determine whether that was truly the case, as Kapuściński only mentions reading Herodotus a couple of times in *Lapidaria*, and not in any other book).

Kapuściński reads *The Histories* over and over again, over the course of many years. During his most fascinating adventures or most exotic journeys, Herodotus becomes Kapuściński's close friend, and always stands by Kapuściński's side, which might be read as a certain cockiness or an exaggerated faith in Kapuściński's own importance. Kapuściński, from the beginning of *Travels*, stresses the importance of Herodotus and sometimes more, sometimes less subtly suggests that he (Kapuściński) wants to be regarded with the same esteem as Herodotus. However, Kapuściński skillfully highlights the distance between himself and Herodotus while simultaneously relying on Herodotus's account in various ways. One of the most striking features of this book is that in Kapuściński's biographical account (contrary to Herodotus' model, where chronology is observed) the narrator does not observe any chronological constraints. This lack of chronological limitation has at least two notable effects: loosening the grip on narration (a rather radical change when compared, for instance, with *The Emperor*) to the point where narration is transformed into a loosely tied account without the narrator intervening in it, and defying time's destructive power by engaging in a "dialogue" with Herodotus.

It could be stated that through this book Kapuściński gives his readers the key to his creation and its often ethically doubtful methods. Already in the first sentence, Kapuściński marks the importance of Herodotus in *Travels*:

---

111 *Travels with Herodotus* was translated into English by Klara Glowczewska and published by Vintage International in New York in 2008. All quotations in this text are from this edition.

Before Herodotus sets out on his travels, ascending rocky paths, sailing a ship over the seas, riding on horseback through the wilds of Asia; before he happens upon the mistrustful Scythians, discovers the wonders of Babylon, and plumbs the mysteries of the Nile; before he experiences a hundred different places and sees a thousand inconceivable things, he will appear for a moment in a lecture on ancient Greece, which Professor Bieżuńska-Małowist delivers twice weekly to the first-year students in Warsaw University's Department of History (7).

A description of Herodotus' appearance during a history lecture placed at the very beginning of the book directs the reader's attention to the crucial place the ancient historian and story teller has in Kapuściński's book. The arrow of time is of little relevance for the narrator and his friend, Herodotus. Herodotus lives outside of time; his travels happen at Kapuściński's narrator's whim, every time he reaches for *The Histories*. Already on the first pages of *Travels*, though, the narrator indicates, Herodotus is the only one who upholds the responsibility toward chronology.

The opening scenes of *Travels* set it far apart from *Imperium* (See Part III Trauma). Even though in *Travels* Kapuściński also mentions his early years (not childhood, though); there is no trauma, fear, or horror. Instead, we constantly encounter a feeling of amazement at the world, even a fascination.

Thus, from the beginning, it is clear that no part of *Travels* plays a similarly therapeutic role for the author, as was the case with parts of *Imperium*. Kapuściński begins by describing a lecture on ancient Greece given by one of his professors at Warsaw University five years after the end of World War II. Polish post-war reality is harsh: there are no books, no supplies, the city is in ruins; Warsaw, which at the end of the war had been completely wiped out by the Germans, is barely alive. The one thing that the University does not lack are students who are eager to learn. The students are accepted to the University without entrance exams, but based on their social class. Even though the opening scenes of *Travels* take place in 1950 when all the atrocities of Stalinism are in full swing, the author implies that the times are gentle, graceful and almost cheerful. Warsaw lies in absolute ruins, the nation is depleted and barely alive, the Secret Police are restless in their hunting of the public enemies, but we find no trace of such dreary socialist-realist existence at the beginning of the book. Instead, the reader's attention is immediately directed toward Herodotus and his momentary appearance in the university classroom:

> The professor has a calm, soft, even voice. Her dark, attentive eyes regard us through thick lenses with marked curiosity. Sitting at a high lectern, she has before her a hundred young people the majority of whom have no idea that Solon was great, do not know the cause of Antigone's despair, and could not explain how Themistocles lured the Persians into a trap. If truth be told, we didn't even quite know where Greece was or, for that matter, that a contemporary country by that

name has a past so remarkable and extraordinary as to merit studying at university. We were children of war. High schools were closed during the war years, and although in larger cities clandestine classes were occasionally convened, here, in this lecture hall, sat mostly girls and boys from remote villages and small towns, ill read, undereducated. [...] The professor showed us photographs of antique sculptures and of Greek figures painted on brown vases – beautiful, statuesque bodies, noble, elongated faces with fine features. They belonged to some unknown, mythic universe, a world of sun and silver, warm and full of light, populated by slender heroes and dancing nymphs. We didn't know what to make of it. [...] Before those future prophets proclaiming the clash of civilizations, the collision was taking place long ago, twice a week, in the lecture hall where I learned that there once lived a Greek named Herodotus (5).

The tone and descriptions of Polish reality in the opening scenes of *Travels* inscribe themselves into accusations directed at Kapuściński for his selective or even creative treatment of facts.[112] The narrator says that in the years immediately following World War II, he and his peers at the university lacked any knowledge about Greece or its ancient past. As a matter of fact, in the years 1946-1949 there was a terrible civil war in Greece, fought between communists and monarchists.[113] The narrator does not mention that as a result of the war around 14,000 Greek refugees came to Poland. The Polish government immediately granted them asylum as repressed communists. Many of the Greek refugees returned to their own country only after the democratic government had been restored in Greece in the 1970s. The case of the Greek communist refugees was well known by the general public, mostly due to the fact that it was heavily publicized by the official media to promote an idea of brotherhood among all communist nations united against the repressive imperialist "juntas." Thus, omitting such well known facts and claiming that his history professor's lectures were happening in a historical and cognitive vacuum Kapuściński sets *Travels* apart as a book with a narrative happening beyond various limitations, and mainly beyond space, time and ideology.[114]

As *Travels* is in a certain way a continuation of *Lapidaria*, it contains the report of a journey into the depths of Kapuściński's own self. From the very beginning of the book, Kapuściński establishes his own central place in the described world. He is at the center, the knowing subject, acting as the lens, the prism, and the hub through which all the information flows, his consciousness is the matrix which arrays the world around him. The book is a testament to him

---

112   Jack Shafer, "The Lies of Ryszard Kapuściński, or, if you prefer, the "magical realism" of the now-departed master," *Slate Magazine*, Jan. 25, 2007.
113   http://pl.wikipedia.org/wiki/Wojna_domowa_w_Grecji
114   I am thankful to Prof. Bożena Shallcross for this observation.

learning about the world and its history and embracing the lives of all the inhabitants of the planet, whether alive or not. The concept of this narrative taking the events of his life beyond the limits of time and space is executed in a light, gentle and almost cheerful way. It has none of the heavy-handed approach of *The Emperor* nor the gloomy mood of failed therapy pervading *Imperium*.

III. Approaching the unknown

Kapuściński's first job was in a heavily propagandist newspaper called *Sztandar Młodych* (*The Banner of Youth*). The newspaper was an organ of Związek Młodzieży Polskiej (ZMP), a Polish communist youth organization active between 1948 and 1957 and modeled on the Soviet Komsomol. ZMP's objective was to indoctrinate the youth in line with the Communist Party's discourse. Both *Sztandar Młodych* and ZMP were symbols of the Polish version of Stalinism. The narrator never mentions the zealous profile of the newspaper and says that he started working at *Sztandar Młodych* in 1955, "Two years had passed since Stalin's death ... I completed my studies and began working at a newspaper. It was called *Sztandar Młodych* (*The Banner of Youth*)" (8). In reality, Kapuściński started working at *Sztandar Młodych* when he was still in high school, that is in 1950, during the apogee of Stalinism. His job consisted of going to villages located in the new post-war, westward-shifted border areas and ascertaining whether the laws and policies of the newly established communist state were being implemented and writing reportage pieces about his experiences.

In *Travels*, in the descriptions of his youth activist trips, Kapuściński, as if to counter the usually heavily politically loaded picture of the 1950s, signals a feeling of mystery and longing. He describes this feeling as a fascination with the mysteriousness of crossing a border:

> My route sometimes took me to villages along the border. But this happened infrequently. For the closer one got to a border, the emptier grew the land and the fewer people one encountered. This emptiness increased the mystery of those regions. I was struck, too, by how salient the border zone was. This mystery and quiet attracted and intrigued me. I was tempted to see what lay beyond on the other side. I wondered what one experiences when one crosses the border. What does one feel? What does one think? It must be a moment of great emotion, agitation, tension. (9)

However, Kapuściński's actual early poetry and reportage pieces published at the beginning of his career in the early 1950s, which was very much in line with the Stalinist rhetoric of the period, created a myth of the New and the Progressive, rather than the Unknown and the Mysterious.[115] Interestingly, rather than being intrigued by what lies on the other side of a border, Kapuściński is mesmerized by the mere process of crossing it. Moreover, in *Travels,* he creates a situation in which he can cross into heterotopia:

---

115 See for example: "Pisane szybkością," *Dziś i jutro* 32, 1949, "Marzenia naiwne," *Dziś i jutro* 6, 1950, "Wielki rzut," *Polityka* 5, 1950, "Rozmowy na ulicy," *Sztandar Młodych* 7, 1957.

> There are also, probably in every culture, in every civilization, real places - places that do exist and that are formed in the very founding of society - which are something like counter-sites, a kind of effectively enacted utopia in which the real sites, all the other real sites that can be found within the culture, are simultaneously represented, contested, and inverted. Places of this kind are outside of all places, even though it may be possible to indicate their location in reality. Because these places are absolutely different from all the sites that they reflect and speak about, I shall call them, by way of contrast to utopias, heterotopias.[116]

Heterotopias could be described as mythic spaces associated with a disjunction in time and rituals preventing unconstrained access to them. Consequently, we could say that the version of borders presented in *Travels* could be treated as heterotopian spaces. Even from the beginning of the book we can argue that Kapuściński attempts a transformation of the events of his life into a heterotopic space of a 'creative biography.'

It should be added that while, in my opinion, seeing borders as heterotopias is acceptable, I do not think we could include them in Jurgen Habermas' notion of public sphere – a place where no ideology operates or where there is no 'representation' – as Kapuściński's borders or his 'creative biography' was a direct result of oppressive ideology at work.

In *Travels* we read that in tightly politically and culturally controlled and religiously homogenous 1950s Poland the author is drawn to those desired and imagined heterotopias. However in reality, precisely because of his uncritical faith in communism, Kapuściński is convinced that history is bound to progress in a limitless and immeasurable way. During the years to come, his faith in communism is severely tested and eventually fades; he finds out that history is not a subject to such simplistic rules and that only being on the road constitutes such free 'heterotopic' space. Moreover, the author realizes that such desire is as old as humanity itself and was well described over 2000 years ago by Herodotus. Kapuściński does not just want to be on the road, he wants to be constantly on the journey through time. In the biography he presents in *Travels*, Kapuściński achieves it through his own travels and by traveling in time with Herodotus.

1. Initiation into the world of reporting

The description of Kapuściński's initial journey as a foreign correspondent to India was first published in English in *The New Yorker* under the title "The

---

116 Michel Foucault, "Des Escapes Autres" (Of Other Spaces), *Architecture/ Mouvement/Continuité*, Paris: October 1984, p. 2.

Open World" on February 7, 2007, before the entire book came out in 2008. In the Polish edition this piece is divided into two chapters titled "Przekroczyć granicę" and "Skazany na Indie." In his typical self-deprecating way Kapuściński writes that during this trip, to his great amazement, he learned that being a foreign correspondent was not going to be just a pleasant vacationing in exotic places but quite a demanding calling with his life often at stake. His first foreign journey turned out to be an exciting, shocking, and humbling encounter with radical Otherness. After having returned home, he perceived the trip to India as a failure:

> India was my first encounter with otherness, the discovery of a new world. It was at the same time a great lesson in humility. [...] I tried to forget India, which signified to me my failure: its enormity and incomprehensibility had crushed, stunned, and finally defeated me (39).

The author, to his great suprprise, learned that he had to put effort into preparing himself for a journey and that a different culture was not simply going to allow him access at a wave of his hand.

After returning from India and trying to forget about his failure, Kapuściński again throw himself into his work at *Sztandar Mlodych*. Since communication with his fellow countrymen is easy, safe, and simply part of his upbringing (little effort is needed), he again travels around Poland just as he had done before the Indian trip. He yet again writes many reportage pieces about the post-war situation in Poland, much within the Party line. But at the same time, in a typical way for someone who is in denial, India is more and more present in his consciousness. In the winter, the snow and frost remind him of the heat in Kerala, while the early sunsets make him think about beautiful sunrises in Kashmir. India slightly undermines in Kapuściński's consciousness his monolithic view of the world but the structure of his ideology and his writing do not change immediately after the trip. The Indian experiences only provide him with a new vantage point.

At the end of his Indian trip description, in a chapter titled "The Train Station and The Palace," Kapuściński writes about his return flight from Moscow to Warsaw. On the plane, he sits next to a tired, old man, who as Kapuściński finds out at the end of the flight had been sent to a gulag in Siberia after the Soviet Union annexed the eastern Polish territories at the beginning of World War II. The old man is now returning home to Poland: "It was December 1956. People were still coming out of the gulags" (38). The ending of the trip to India is a fairy-tale ending: the poor old prisoner is now coming back home. In reality, former gulag prisoners were usually not allowed to travel on planes or, more often, they simply could not afford air travel; usually their narratives describe months-long train trips. In Kapuściński's story, however, a young enthusiastic reporter, actively participating in history *in statu nascendi*, traveling around the globe meets a ghost from the dark past. The fairy-tale ending happens for a reason: the author has to meet a former gulag prisoner returning home, so he (the author) can highlight the fact that Stalinism is over and a new era of the world's history is beginning – an era in which Third World countries will play a more and more important role as they free themselves from colonialism. Moreover, through Kapuściński's unusual encounter, we are made aware that history is actually a meeting point of many histories, all of which are present and active. The moment of the encounter also becomes a true clash of worlds and Kapuściński's initiation into the world of reporting, which is going to be precisely such negotiation between not two but many worlds at the same time.

Travels contains many other descriptions of Kapuściński's reportorial firsts. One of the earliest forays he describes is the first coup d'etat in post-war Africa, which, as the rest of the 20th century proved, turned out to be the first in a line of many coups. Kapuściński describes his unexpected visit to Algiers in 1965: he arrives in Algiers the day after the coup, in which Ben Bella had been removed and Houari Bumedien installed. Kapuściński searches the city for signs of trouble, trauma, riots, street fights, etc., but he finds none of them in Algiers. The city functions in its ordinary way, as if nothing had happened. He begins to understand that often the biggest political changes do not happen in a belligerent way, and that people in the streets do not acknowledge the upper class political reshuffling. Kapuściński's experience of witnessing the coup in Algiers is an important element of his learning process, not just in the sense of widening his knowledge of the world, but of himself as well. Alongside becoming a more experienced reporter, he is learning about himself and his process of cognition. He slowly changes from a provincial, young, simple-minded, and naïve local journalist into an increasingly experienced, savvy, worldly, and confident reporter.

Another aspect of the initiation into the life of reporting Kapuściński describes is the physicality of his profession. Experiencing the world somatically attributes an ethnographic authority to him.

> This is possible because of [his] ethnographic authority ... consisting of three structural elements: an ethnographic signature of "being there," traces of personal experience, and an anti-tourist attitude, often affirmed by the writer *expressis verbis*. [Kapuściński] was aware that it is neither conceptual elegance nor extensive description which persuades the reader to an ethnographic text/reportage, but rather a dexterity in convincing him/her that a particular text is the result of realistically distorting a different way of life, the result of "being there."[117]

---

117 Paweł Zajas, "Zagubieni kosmonauci. Raz jeszcze o *Imperium* Ryszarda Kapuścińskiego i jego krytykach" ("Lost Cosmonauts: On Ryszard Kapuscinski's *Imperium* and Its Critics – Once More"), *Teksty Drugie* (3: 2010): 218-231.

Kapuściński's trips demanded an enormous physical effort, made apparent early in the story:

> I reached China on foot. I flew to Hong Kong via Amsterdam and Tokyo. In Honk Kong, a local train took me to a small station in an open field – where, I had been told, I would be able to cross into China. In reality, however, when I stepped down onto the platform, it was only to be approached by a conductor and a policeman, who gestured toward a bridge on the far horizon. "China!" the policeman said. He was a Chinese man in a British police uniform. He walked with me a ways along the asphalt road, then wished me a good journey and turned back for the station. I continued on alone, carrying my suitcase in one hand and a bag full of books in the other. The sun beat down mercilessly, the air was hot and heavy, flies buzzed aggressively. The bridge was short, with a diagonal metal grating, and below it flowed a half dried-up river. [...] Guards [...] told me to keep walking—toward a train which was visible perhaps half a kilometer away. I walked on in the heat, with great effort, perspiring, amidst swarms of flies (53).

The moment of crossing the Hong Kong-Chinese border is described as if it were shown through a camera with a fish-eye lens: everything is magnified and happens in slow motion. Here, in this creative moment appropriation, creativity is closely connected with the presence of the body and its limitations. The world is perceived through oneself, as Kapuściński often absorbs the reality around him through his own body. We often read that he is tired, thirsty, that he gets offered pieces of pork fat by a fellow passenger on a train to Moscow (*Imperium*, 275), that he is dizzy while driving through the desert (*Shadow of the Sun*, 52), or that he experiences intense and strange emotions when he smokes hashish, and the next day he is terribly hung-over (*Travels*, 121). His own physicality grows to be a crucial presence in his books and serves to establish and enforce his ethnographic authority.

2. Difficult Otherness

During his first trip to India, Kapuściński constantly runs into the wall of misunderstanding. He cannot even speak English. In order to start communicating he starts learning English from a Hemingway book; the prose so clear and precise that one wonders how Kapuściński cannot understand it: "He lay flat on the brown, pine-needled floor of the forest, his chin on his folded arms, and high overhead the wind blew in the tops of pine trees."[118] Not knowing the language of the colonizers makes him feel closer to most people in India who are equally marginalized, as most natives do not speak English either. However, he himself

---

118 Ernest Hemingway, *For Whom the Bell Tolls*, quoted after Kapuściński, *Travels*, p. 20.

notices that he is worried about not speaking *English*, but does not worry about not speaking any of the indigenous languages, like Hindi, Bengali, Urdu, Tamil, Punjabi – he is conscious of the colonizers' conceptual net imposed upon India and his own cognitive process being trapped by that net. While in India, Kapuściński struggles with not being able to understand anything around him; language becomes something physical and material, standing between him and the world. It prevents him from cognition. It makes him feel foreign, strange, not belonging. "I understood that every distinct geographic universe has its own mystery and that one can decipher it only by learning the local language" (22).

During that trip, Kapuściński is 24 years old. He is a young man from a communist country, where history had been taking extreme turns, displacing and uprooting millions of people. In India, he is faced with a culture, which went uninterrupted (except for the British colonization) for thousands of years and where most people did not know or did not care at all about Poland's problems, which to Kapuściński seem absolutely crucial. His outlook on the world had been shaped by rationalism and materialism, and before that by the horrors of the war. His world, mindset, and culture are a galaxy away from what he encounters on the Indian subcontinent. Nothing is familiar, there is nothing that he could use as a starting point in acclimating himself to India. There is not even a common language. He experiences an almost physical sensation of being severed from the world around him.

> I felt trapped. Besieged by language. Language struck me at that moment as something material, something with a physical dimension, a wall rising up in the middle of the road and preventing my going further, closing off the world, making it unattainable. It was an unpleasant and humiliating sensation. It might explain why, in a first encounter with someone or someone foreign, there are those who will fear and uncertainty, bristle with mistrust. What will this meeting bring? Who will it end? Better not to risk it and to remain in the cocoon of the familiar? Better not to stick one's neck out of one's own backyard! (20)

Such obstacles in learning about a culture lead to a burning desire to simplify the incomprehensible reality surrounding the narrator – meeting the Other is, after all, like exploring another planet. Through his own example, Kapuściński shows how extraordinarily difficult it is to comprehend a different culture, and how easily one resorts to oversimplifying and disrespecting it. And sure enough, in "Condemned to India" and the subsequent three chapters on China, we encounter various, often shocking oversimplifications.

> But the Great Wall was only a metaphor—a symbol and a sign, the coat of arms and the escutcheon of what had been a nation of walls for millennia. The Great Wall demarcated the empire's northern borders but walls were also erected between warring principalities, between regions and even neighborhoods. The structures defend-

ed cities and villages, passes and bridges. They guarded palaces, government buildings, temples, and markets. Barracks, police stations, and prisons. Wall encircled private home, separated neighbor form neighbor, family from family. If one assumes that the Chinese built walls uninterruptedly for hundreds, even thousands of years, and if one factors in the population—enormous throughout the national history— their dedication and devotion - their exemplary discipline and purposefulness, then one reckons with hundreds upon hundreds of millions of hours spent building walls, hours which in this poor country could have been spent learning to read, acquiring a profession, cultivation new fields, and breeding robust cattle (58).

Although the Hindu and the Chinese writing systems caused me a great difficulty, the behavior of people in the two countries could not have been more different. The Hindu is a relaxed being, while the Chinese is a tense and vigilant one. A crowd of Hindus is formless, fluid, slow; a crowd of Chinese is formed before you know it into disciplined marching lines. One senses that above a gathering of Chinese stands a commander, a higher authority, while above the multitude of Hindus hovers an Aeropagus of innumerable and undemanding deities. If a throng of Hindus encounters something interesting, it stops, looks, and begins discussing. In a similar situation, the Chinese will walk on, in close formation, obedient, their eyes fixed on a designated goal (65).

Are such oversimplifications here to make the comprehension of these two huge civilizations easier? Are they supposed to prove that one cannot comprehend the radical Other without reducing him or her to one's pre-shaped concepts? If so, the effort which has to be undertaken in getting to know the Other is so enormous that few people can rise to it. Kapuściński is convinced that he and Herodotus can be counted among such people, but even they, as the chapters on India and China exemplify, cannot escape the trap of reducing the unknown into the familiar.

There are numerous other unknown matters Kapuściński discovers when he tries to make contact with the local culture. The language barrier is the most obvious impediment, also likely the most painful one. But of course, it is not just the language that prevents him from understanding India. One of the first trips he undertakes after having arrived in Delhi is to the "sacred town" of Benares. There, he experiences a truly drastic otherness. He observes people pouring human ashes into the Ganges River, where, at the same time, other people are taking ritual baths – something that for him is absolutely incomprehensible, while for the local residents, who recommend visiting that town, is a beautiful ritual. Kapuściński does not understand it, lacking the historical, cultural and religious background tools for the endeavor. He also lacks a sense of the sacred; his mindset had been shaped by rationalism and Marxism and does not allow room for sacrum. The ritual he witnesses in Benares, which for thousands of people is an amazing spiritual experience, remains for him only an empty ceremony. For

Kapuściński, only the moment of crossing a border carries the aura of mystery. A sense of the sacred is completely absent from his text. Correspondingly, Kapuściński notices that after having read Herodotus' *Histories* for the first time, he is struck by the absence of sacrum and the language that often accompanies it – language that is lofty, elevated, and highly symbolic. In Herodotus' world, there are no gods intervening from the heavens; people are left to their own devices. Herodotus even goes so far as to discuss questions of the gods' origin. There is no lingua sacra invading his discourse, just a basic, solid discussion: who did it, who *invented* the gods: the Greeks or the Egyptians? Herodotus does not wonder whose gods are the greatest, mightiest, or oldest, but inquires about their source. Similarly for Kapuściński, when he describes the ritual he witnessed in Benares, India, he sees only a strange, spectacular rite deprived of sacred elements. Moreover, not only is there no description of any superior being to whom the ritual is addressed, but also no spiritual bond with the people performing that ritual.

On another day, the first time the author goes out on his own into the streets of Delhi, the rickshaw drivers want to offer him their services, but he proudly refuses, thinking highly of himself (i.e. that he does not take advantage of poor, ill-fed people); in fact, he denies the men the only opportunity to earn money. This Otherness, even though desired by him, turns out to be something very precarious – difficult to comprehend and to embrace. He discovers, again and again, that learning about the Other is not just pleasure and amazement, but a process which has to be undertaken constantly and diligently. And through this, his famous egalitarianism becomes genuine.

3. Juxtapositions

In the descriptions of his first two trips to India and China, Kapuściński often (if not overtly) uses juxtaposition; the two countries are placed on opposite sides of his reportorial spectrum. At the same time, even though juxtaposed, both countries are very different from 1950's Poland. Pitting two countries/concepts in direct opposition builds a dialectical tension, which Kapuściński then uses to structure the story.

The trip to India becomes an allegory of oppositions: Poland and India. India becomes a synonym of abundance of everything, including religion. Kapuściński finds, to his great astonishment, that in Hinduism there are endless ways to salvation, paths of virtue, practices of chastity and asceticism, etc. The sacred Indian books are significantly bigger, older and longer than the Judeo-Christian religious texts. There are dozens of ways to practice and understand

Hindu philosophy. For Kapuściński, a person raised under one state-imposed philosophy and one church-established religion, this abundance and endlessness is a shock. The way the author presents his assignment in India as almost allegorical. In Kapuściński's 1950s Poland everything is scarce, from food to buildings to ideas; even color is a rarity as everything in post-war communist reality is grey and drab. In India, everything is as colorful and as plentiful as possible. However, while undoubtedly Poland was enormously damaged after World War II, not all the historical buildings and structures were destroyed: the Poland of the Romanesque, Gothic, Renaissance, Baroque and other historical and colorful periods still exists. This alleged lack of color in postwar Poland is a political creation of the imagination of Polish dissidents; it is present for instance in Tadeusz Konwicki's writing. Does Kapuściński, while re-creating his biography, try to inscribe himself into that trend as well?

Both China and India provide proof of Kapuściński's early reportorial ignorance. At first glance, China's only function in the text seems to be juxtaposition with India. In Kapuściński's China, an inaccessible mindset is prevalent; as a result he presents China in an inadequate and fragmentary way. Most of his stay in China is filled with attempts to acquire insight into the lives and thoughts of his hosts, while they, for their part, attempt all manner of evasion. Unlike in India, he and his hosts share a common language – Russian – but that does not help them to effectively communicate. This failed attempt at communication on any level other than just mere verbal exchange thwarts Kapuściński's understanding of China. In one description after another, he proves that after he had initially seen China through a one-dimensional metaphor, that is The Great Wall as a wall of a huge prison, and it is difficult for him to shake these initial perceptions. As if this inaccessible Chinese mindset he describes is actually his own and inhibits him from learning more about this diverse and complicated country.

During Kapuściński's journey from Hong Kong to mainland China, he notices – to his great astonishment – that everyone on his train looks, dresses, and behaves alike (54). He seems to be uncomfortable with the fact that no one on the train notices him, or at least people behave as if they do not see him. However, this indifference to a foreigner should not be surprising to a person from a communist country, where a great level of control was exercised over all aspects of life. The Chinese people *must* have noticed him, most likely they were simply afraid or trained not to express any kind of emotions. The situation was arguably not much different from Poland in the early 1950s where having contact with a foreigner was also looked upon with suspicion by the authorities and for many ended in jail time. Yet, Kapuściński does not reflect upon the situation or attempt to understand the position of the people on the train; he is merely astonished and even slightly indignant.

Being a young, naïve rookie reporter, ill-read, unprepared, coming from a closed-off country, Kapuściński is forced by his lack of knowledge to adopt an overly simplistic view of the two countries he visits at the early years of his career. Thus, when considering India and China, he conveniently portrays them to fit his own model: India is open and accepting, while China is inaccessible and vigilant. These two magnificent, diverse, and ancient cultures yield only one thing to Kapuściński: they are both equally unknowable to him.

4. Lack of chronology

In the description of his reportorial beginnings, Kapuściński transitions directly from writing reports for *Sztandar Młodych* to being informed by his editor of his trip to India (14). However, there is a chronological break in his story: that is his Nowa Huta article.[119] As Michał Głowiński states, "that which remains unsaid becomes a structural element of the novel."[120] The fact that Kapuściński chooses to exclude the reasons for being sent abroad is telling – he does not feel an obligation to adhere to chronology in order to keep the story together; he can omit important events, even those that provide the impetus for his travels (which is ultimately the Nowa Huta article's agency – it was the direct cause mandating him to briefly leave Poland, escaping the radar of the authorities). Instead, Kapuściński 'employs' Herodotus to maintain the order of the story in his stead. As a consequence, Kapuściński does not have to stick tightly to the facts; he can utilize a narrative mode of writing, enabling him to stray from a dry, verbatim report. *Travels* is considerably more invested in the aesthetics of narrative than in merely relating facts.

At the same time, Kapuściński often reminds the reader that Herodotus does not practice the fact-gripping type of writing either, and that he (Herodotus) should not be reproached for not relating purely facts. The only significant element, Kapuściński claims, is that Herodotus travels extensively and undertakes an enormous cognitive and physical effort, which later results in a skillfully constructed book. Kapuściński wants a similar reputation for himself: respect for his efforts, understanding of the demands of story-telling, and no reproof for not stringently reporting only dry facts. In "The Face of Zopyros" Herodotus presents the story of Zopyros, Darius' adviser, who mutilates his own face to guilt Darius into attacking Babylon (130). It is a horrible story, similar to murdering

---

119 I describe Kapuściński's exposé of Nowa Huta and the consequences of it in Part I Introduction on page 22.
120 Michał Głowiński, *Gry powieściowe: Szkice z teorii i historii form narracyjnych*, Warszawa: PWN, 1973, p. 28 (my translation).

tens of thousands of women and children of Babylon (so they would not eat the food reserves in the city besieged by Persians). However, Kapuściński presents these stories from Herodotus' account without questioning the validity of the latter's reporting or how true the stories really were. Kapuściński leaves the questioning to the readers.

In Kapuściński's view, Herodotus freely mixes related facts with overheard rumors, unbelievable dreams and fantastic myths. Herodotus does not assign a higher value to either discourse, as he realizes that both real and fictional discourses can equally efficiently create real-life situations: if a king tells his subjects that he had a dream in which a ghost told him to start a war, his subjects will not question him when he starts a war. Kapuściński then cites Herodotus in order to deem non-factual discourse to be as important as any other discourse.

This lack of chronological constraints results in the book's discourse becoming increasingly reflexive and gentle. Kapuściński relinquishes control over the narrative to such an extent that he ceases to observe chronology. He does not finish his story or give the full details or mechanisms behind the events. The narrator of *Travels*, unlike the narrator of *The Emperor*, does not have authoritarian inclinations and leaves the story's axis, chronology, and coherence to Herodotus. No carefully delineated distance exists between Kapuściński and his narrator. Agency is in turn transposed onto Herodotus – he is the one who keeps watch over the coherence of Kapuściński's story. Consequently, the present-tense narration is subject to the order of events from over 2000 years ago.

This radical narrative choice left many reviewers of *Travels With Herodotus* rather surprised:

> Long-term admirers of Ryszard Kapuściński may be disappointed to learn that in *Travels with Herodotus*, his last work, the Polish journalist and writer is mellower, kinder, warmer than in books published in the spit and fury of his younger years. The opening lines ... lack the rawness of those other works.[121]

> There is distressingly little to argue over in *Travels With Herodotus*. The narrative floats about like an uncaptained trireme ... and the pectorals of his language have lost some definition ... The sorcerer casts a few enchantments in *Travels With Herodotus*, but only one of them comes within range of either of the above [that is of *Shah of Shahs* and *Another Day of Life*].[122]

Other reviews stated that Kapuściński "lost his edge," and that *Travels* lacks the "horrific immediacy" of his earlier and more shocking books. The reviewers,

---

121 Jason Burke, "Beyond the Spectacle," http://www.literaryreview.co.uk/burke_06_07.html
122 Tom Bissel, "On the Road with History's Father," *New York Times*, June 10, 2007.

however, do not seem to notice that loosening the narrator's grip is a deliberate move – exchanging the narrator's control for an unfettered narrative. Unlike most of his earlier books, *Travels* is not a controversial story inspired by sensational events in political hotspots of the world, but it is a creative synthesis of the author's life.

During his eventful trip to Iran in 1979 (whose result was *Shah of Shahs*), Kapuściński leaves action-packed Tehran for a while and goes on a short trip to Persepolis, the city of "dead kings and forgotten gods" (148). Kapuściński's visit to Persepolis is directly inspired by *The Histories* and the influential dynasty of the Achaemenid. The description of Kapuściński's visit to the tranquil ancient capital is captivating, and its mood is set against the hectic atmosphere of the current capital of Persia. When he leaves Persepolis, the ancient city quickly blends with the horizon, dead, forgotten, abandoned. Shortly thereafter Kapuściński is back in Tehran, in a political hotspot, where the revolution is at its peak, and the streets are full of shouting crowds, noisy riots, and deafening shots. This is yet another situation through which he shows how his curiosity and insatiable need for learning leads him to exist in several epochs simultaneously.

> I left Persepolis and now I am leaving Tehran, going back twenty years and returning once more to Africa. But along the way I must stop—in my thoughts, that is—in the Greco-Persian world of Herodotus, for dark clouds are beginning to gather over it (155).

Herodotus becomes Kapuściński's companion and friend during the years of traveling alongside the author of *Travels*. Kapuściński even confesses to sometimes identifying more with Herodotus' world than his own, which in turn can be explained by Kapuściński's desire to experience other times than his own fast-paced world.

In an essay on Virgil written in 1944, T.S. Eliot warns his readers about the provincialism of time:

> When men seem more than ever prone to confuse wisdom with knowledge, and knowledge with information, and to try to solve the problems of life in terms of engineering, there is coming into existence a new kind of provincialism which perhaps deserves a new name. It is a provincialism, not of space, but of time; one for which history is merely the chronicle of human devices which have served their turn and been scrapped, one for which the world is the property solely of the living, a property in which the dead hold no shares. The menace of this kind of provincialism is, that we can all, all the peoples on the globe, be provincials together; and those who are not content to be provincials, can only become hermits.[123]

---

123 Quoted after Kapuściński, *Travels*, p. 254.

According to Eliot and Kapuściński, a provincial mindset can exist in two varieties: provincialism of space and of time. Each globe shows the provincial of space that their piece of land does not comprise the center of the world. The provincials of time, however, have to be constantly reminded that their events merely belong to a long timeline of human history, and that the present has always existed: "history is merely an uninterrupted progression of presents, that what for us are ancient events were for those who lived them immediate for present reality" (256). In the version of his life presented in *Travels*, Kapuściński always travels with a copy of Herodotus' book at his side to ward off temporal provincialism. Only with Herodotus as his constant companion is he able to comprehend reality as an uninterrupted continuation of yesterday and a preparation for tomorrow. It should be added though that such comprehension of reality warrants a condition: invention often replacing faithfulness to the facts.

In the late 1960s while in Africa, Kapuściński takes a short vacation from his typically intensive reporting duties and ventures to the lakes of Abaya and Chamo in Ethiopia. This short vacation is unusually quiet and relaxed for him. He reads Herodotus' description of dark clouds gathering above the world: Xerxes is mustering a war effort against Greece. The war is one of the greatest of that time, and it has an enormous impact on the entire known world. While Xerxes is preparing for war, Kapuściński's vacation ends and he has to go back to Addis Ababa. Both stories run parallel and influence one another; Kapuściński does not heed any chronological disjunction, thus there are no temporal distinctions between 480 BC and the 1960s.

> In the morning, a peasant woman in a white robe sets up on the verandah a wooden armchair, as well a massive sculpted wooden table. Silence, water, several acacia trees, and in the far distance, in the background, the gigantic, dark green Amaro mountains. One feels like the king of the world here. I've brought with me a bundle of periodicals with articles about Africa, but from time to time I also reach for the tome from which I am inseparable [...] I can see that serious and dangerous things are happening in my Greek's world, I sense a historic storm brewing, a sinister hurricane approaching (189).

The atemporal aspect of telling a story provided for Kapuściński by Herodotus, allows the former to acquire prophetic skills. Inspired by Herodotus, he sees into the future. The historical storm brewing is actually going to soon happen in Addis Abbaba where the Ehtiopian college students and peasants will rebel against Haile Sellassie. While an interesting literary device, it might be questioned whether forestalling of events has a place in journalism. It does, however, have place in fiction or creative writing.

IV. Egalitarianism

While reading about ancient civilizations and visiting the ruins of early cities, Kapuściński relates his experiences to contemporary events. As he zealously serves the communist system, he also acquires an intimate knowledge of it and often undermines many comfortable notions. Kapuściński mentions The Great Wall of China and the City of Persepolis as examples of ancient, ethically questionable greatness. For him, the Great Wall of China is not a wonder, rather it is

> [...] a proof of a kind of human weakness, of an aberration, of a horrifying mistake; it is evidence of a historical inability of people in this part of the planet to communicate, to confer and jointly determine how best to deploy enormous reserves of human energy and intellect (62).

In his eyes, a wonder of the world is a symbol of wasted lives, violence, and slavery as well as proof that many great civilizations are built on the deaths of their slaves. Another example of ethically questionable magnitude is Persepolis, a city brought to its greatness by the Achaemenid dynasty. "How often do we consider the fact that the treasures and riches of the world were created from time immemorial by slaves?" (227). He gives voice to those who are denied one; he praises the unknown builders of the city, their sweat, pain, broken backs, and the enormous amount of labor put into processing the stones. He is determined to remind the reader that tyrannies produce beautiful and daunting monuments, which are eventually forgotten or abandoned. They are the epitome of superfluously wasted energy, yet they are very impressive monuments of the past. In such statements, his genuine egalitarianism shines through the text and reminds the reader that despite his ethically questionable treatment of facts, Kapuściński is a creator of truly great stories.

Herodotus chooses to write his book about the Greek-Persian wars because in his opinion it is the crucial event influencing the course of history in his times (245). For Kapuściński, the crucial event of his lifetime is the end of colonialism and all the resultant events. Herodotus tirelessly gathers facts, material, and news. He discovers even then that memory is not a stable quality, that people remember what they *want* to remember, and that everyone has their own version of facts. Memory and past are simply constructions of the mind shared by many, or sometimes only shared by some. At the same time, creating memory is our responsibility and has to be handled with great care: lacking knowledge of the past means not existing (206). Herodotus' great concern is the issue of storing knowledge and then sharing it with his peers and successive generations. He realizes that knowledge left unshared is not just useless but also dangerous since it can be easily abused as a tool for any kind of oppressive ideology.

An important theme appearing in all parts of the book is the dichotomy of tyranny and democracy. Kapuściński and Herodotus both say that democracy is a system in which the discourse of control does not prevail. Both authors conclude that the possibility of change and diversity exist only in democracy, as there is no room for change or growth in the closed, hermetic system of tyranny. An inextricable element of authoritarian systems of power is the discourse of control. It, in turn, leads to creating a very dangerous "postawa obrońcy muru," which Klara Glowczewska translates as "it is to turn so many people into defenders [of a wall];" however, in my opinion "the demeanor of a wall defender" would be more accurate. "Obrońca muru" (a wall defender) is a person who stands guard at the "wall," who becomes a firm believer in the system, invents reasons for its existence (often raising these reasons to the level of religion) and demands an absolute obedience to those reasons from people kept inside the wall. People with "postawa obrońcy muru" are perfect subjects of a tyrannical system, since it is most often through them and their zealous servility (not through the tyrant himself) that the system is sustained. Such people and their "postawa obrońcy muru" allow tyrannies to flourish. Counterpoised to such demeanor is an approach of openness and sharing knowledge practiced for instance, as Kapuściński presents it, by Herodotus. Herodotus' approach to gathering knowledge about the world is grassroots, diegetic and horizontal, done through careful observation and active participation (164). Only through such an approach and a constant exchange of knowledge and memory can we negate and avoid the deceptiveness and unreliability of a falsified version of reality. And for this reason, both authors claim they write their books, for they want to share their knowledge with as many as possible.

5. Collective effort of reportage

Kapuściński's view of reportage is that it is a 'democratic,' collective genre which undergoes constant change. For this reason, it has the capability of escaping the limitations inscribed in each clearly defined literary genre. Reportage, in spite of its recently gained popularity and recognition, is still quite peripheral. According to Homi Bhabha, only peripheries do not subscribe to the main discourse of control, as

> [o]nly from the margins can one perform one's ethical duty as an intellectual, in part because one's duty is to represent and advocate the interests of the marginalized, the dispossessed, the underrepresented. ... The margin is actually more central than the centre. ... If the law of the margin could be shown to regulate the entire field, including the center – where because of repressions, it could not appear – then a cer-

tain dominant configuration of forces would be overturned and the world would become open to new kinds of agency.[124]

In Kapuściński's view reportage is a literary genre whose salient feature is its collective creation (170). Both Herodotus' and Kapuściński's books are, in the opinion of the author of *Travels*, results of a collective effort. The stories the authors recount are generated by the people and by the relationships the authors forge with people (173). Kapuściński reminds us that many of Herodotus' reviewers criticized Herodotus' actual knowledge and the veracity of his facts. The author of *Travels* points out, however, that Herodotus' critics do not mention *how* Herodotus wove his extensive and prolific tapestry. This is, of course, a direct allusion to Kapuściński's own method: the precision of dry facts is not of prime importance, but rather it is the cooperation with people and the collectiveness that carry the biggest significance.

6. Identification with Herodotus

Throughout the book, Kapuściński showcases Herodotus' technique, which serves him to present his own methods, approach, and attitude. Herodotus (or rather Kapuściński's version of Herodotus) does what Kapuściński attempts much later: he presents the strange and often shocking traditions, lifestyles, and rituals without commentary and is often reserved about his sources: "as I've heard, as I've seen, as I was told." Herodotus' job is to bring the message, to be a witness, to translate cultures (178). Herodotus constantly emphasizes his distance, irony, and skepticism; he is often critical; he scoffs, ridicules, and is certainly not naïve. At the same time, Herodotus is not blasé – he is still amazed and delighted, most often at the abundance of peoples and the beauty of nature. In this regard, Herodotus resembles Kapuściński, or rather Kapuściński resembles Herodotus.

Kapuściński's first trip to Algiers in 1965 (the first African coup d'etat he witnessed) leads him also to his first encounter with the Mediterranean Sea, The description of the city and the sea is charming and resembles the mood of Kapuściński's descriptions of Herodotus' native land:

> At the very bottom was the port district, with simple wooden bars all in a row, smelling of fish, wine and coffee. But it was the tart scent of the sea that was most noticeable, a gentle, calming refreshment carried on each gust of the wind. I had never been

---

124 Homi Bhabha, quoted after Geoffrey Galt Harpham, "Imagining the Centre," in: *Critical Ethics: Text, Theory and Responsibility*, ed. Dominic Rainsford and Tim Woods, New York: St. Martin's Press, 1999, p. 38.

in a city where nature is so kind to man. For it offered everything all at once – the sun, a cooling breeze, the brightness of the air, the silver of the sea... (218)

The atmosphere, identical for the descriptions of both Algiers and of Greece, is not chosen accidentally. In the time spent at the Mediterranean Sea during the trip to Morocco Kapuściński comes closer to Herodotus and makes him understand the Greek writer-reporter even better.

Throughout the book, Kapuściński expresses his admiration for Herodotus' courage and boldness, and the conviction the author of *The Histories* had about the importance of his mission (205). Kapuściński even goes so far as to confess a certain attachment to Herodotus, which had formed between them over the years. According to Kapuściński, by having decided to write *The Histories*, Herodotus had initiated a new approach to history. Herodotus was no longer simply a chronicler of the local events but a historian for all humanity, the first globalist. Even though Herodotus did not have today's technology at his disposal, he had visited every nook and cranny of the known world. His achievements are not in any way less impressive than Kapuściński's.

Even though reportage is the result of a collective effort, it nonetheless demands a reporter – an unusually curious but fully dedicated person, whose profession effects a complicated family situation. Both Herodotus and Kapuściński travel extensively and are closer with people whom they meet on the road than their own families (80). Kapuściński esteems such drive and penchant for travel and adventures a kind of illness, which reveals itself as loneliness (253). The insatiable drive to learn as much as possible constantly forces the writers to go increasingly further and damages long-term, more standard human relations. Neither Herodotus nor Kapuściński has one favorite country, or a favorite people; they simply want to remain in a state of travel, which for them becomes a cognitive process. Journey, says Kapuściński, is the answer to many questions – while on the road, the writers create their own map of the world and change it through constant learning (243). The language of the immediate, spoken, Socratic tradition, which Kapuściński favors, requires him to be in constant contact with the people he engages and with the characters he creates.

Kapuściński has endless praise for Herodotus and is amazed by his resilience, perseverance and courage. It can be said that by listing all Herodotus' praises, Kapuściński in effect directs the reader's attention to Kapuściński himself, to his own endless achievements, experiences, and journeys. Kapuściński most likely would have wished for the same kind of appreciation from his readers as he shows for Herodotus.

V. Self-critique

> What moved me most, however, was one of the museum's dark chambers, mysterious as a murky cave, in which, on tables, in display cabinets, and on shelves lie illuminated glass objects which had been pulled up from the depths—cups, bowls, pitchers, perfume flasks, goblets. They are not clearly visible at first, when the doors to the room are still open and daylight penetrates its interior. But when the doors close and it grows dark, the curator presses a switch turning on small light bulbs inside little vessels, bringing to life the fragile, matte pieces of glass, which start to sparkle, brighten, pulsate. We stand in deep, thick darkness, as if at the bottom of the sea, as a feast of Poseidon's, surrounded by goddesses each holding an olive oil lamp above her head.
> We stand in darkness, surrounded by light.
>
> (the final chapter of *Travels*,
> "We stand in darkness, surrounded by light," 275)

Throughout the work, Kapuściński relentlessly reminds the reader that the present is just a meeting point of many presents, and history is simply a construction that never ceases to be constructed. Precisely for that reason, *Travels* does not have a concluding chapter, nor any summarizing remarks or conclusive statements wrapping up the narrative of the book. Kapuściński's linear and orderly relation of Herodotus' *The Histories* concludes at the end of *Travels*. In contrast to *The Histories*, the last scene of *Travels* contains an inconclusive description of Kapuściński's visit to Turkey. Moreover, there are no events in Kapuściński's life or in the timeline of his travels, other than the logic of Herodotus' story, delineating the narrative of *Travels*. Even though *Travels* is, in a sense, an autobiographical book, Kapuściński does not feel compelled to continue relating the rest of his own journeys and adventures after concluding the retelling of Herodotus' story. With the progression of *Travels*, its discourse becomes gradually more self-reflexive and self-directed only to disappear completely at the end of the book. Thus Kapuściński identifies with and relies on Herodotus to a very high degree – it is only Herodotus that gives *Travels* structure, since Kapuściński lets go of the narrator's tyranny almost entirely.

7. Creative autobiography and farewell to ideology

Ascribing crucial significance to an individual and his or her story may be read as Kapuściński's reluctant confession: for a long time, he perceived history as a paradigm for immense sociological changes or an over-arching metaphor for shifting political formations. In his defense, it should be mentioned that even at the beginning of his career, genuine empathy and egalitarianism caused him to see that just one person's story carried the greatest significance, hence his interest in simple people, trivial events, and everyday occurrences. Not everything in Kapuściński's writing was dictated by ideology; he was truly interested in day to day lives of simple people. However, in this book, influenced by Herodotus and his focus on an individual fate, Kapuściński finally admits to the ever-present ideological layer accompanying his vantage of the big picture.

According to Kapuściński, Herodotus never blames one person for his or her flaws and sins but rather condemns a system that is formed in the wrong way. Herodotus, or rather Kapuściński through Herodotus, is a fervent supporter of freedom and democracy, an opponent of autocracy and tyranny. It is the actual person who puts everything at risk, who struggles, falls, and rises again. It is the individual who deserves the greatest praise:

> He [Herodotus] does not blame the human being, but blames the system; it is not the individual who is by nature evil, depraved, villainous—it is the social arrangement in which he happens to live that is evil. That is why Herodotus is a passionate advocate of freedom and democracy and a foe of despotism, authoritarianism, and tyranny—he believes that only under the former circumstances does man have a chance to act with dignity, to be himself, to be human (260).

Even though Kapuściński often perceives the world through the lenses of bigger, long-term historical formations, he, like Herodotus, always praises the individual. In Herodotus (and through him, in Kapuściński), this belief in the individual's central place in the universe may be an influence of the theater of antiquity. Herodotus' book was written during the golden era of ancient theatre, which included giants such as Aeschylus, Sophocles and Euripides. The history of the world (Herodotus' world) is shown through individual fates. The tragic element (tragedy in the sense of individuals having to contend with their fates and being responsible for it but not having direct impact on it) is apparent here. Even though the gods decide what will happen and determine an individual's fate, people have to face their fates individually, not in groups, not as parts of nations or systems.

> Jarda [Kapuściński's Czech friend], who read the Greek long ago and says that he remembers little, asks what struck me most about his book. I answer that it is its tragic dimension. Herodotus was the contemporary of the greatest Greek tragedians—Aeschylus, Sophocles (with whom he may have been personally acquainted), and Euripides. [...] This affected how Greeks wrote, how Herodotus wrote. He explains the history of the world through the fortunes if individuals. The pages of his book, whose goal is the recording of human history, are full of flesh-and-blood people, specific human beings with specific names, who are either powerful or weak, kind of cruel, triumphant or despondent (261).

Herodotus is then defined as a historian but also a teller of fictional stories. In the spirit of Johann Wolfgang von Goethe's *Dichtung und Wahrheit*, invention and truth, Kapuściński presents himself as the Herodotus of our times.

The crucial element of the master narrative of Kapuściński's reportage books is a direct engagement with an underprivileged community. In this type of writing then, the ethical aspect and the epistemological responsibility of the author toward the represented community should remain the central element. A traditionally understood reporting is based on a temporal and spatial immediacy of events and is strict in its fact-gripping. Yet, the discourses of most of Kapuściński's books are creations that are not closely tied to reality; in his books the facts are made to serve a purpose, they are carefully chosen and cut to shape. Throughout *Travels* and his other books as well, Kapuściński consciously maintains his image as a trusting and gullible traveler. The meek and mellow attitude is yet another way of aligning himself with the "subaltern," with the seemingly random simple people he meets and describes. Through the creation of his literary alter ego, he asserts the association with the Third World, and opposes the First World, and – supported by it – tyranny. For decades Kapuściński's sense of tyranny was directed only at tyranny that was not tied to communism. Most of his reflections on poverty and exploitation were done from the position of a true believer in communism and a harsh critic of the generally understood "West." The author's personality was also a curious mixture of incredible bravery and disturbing spinelessness. Kapuściński, along with decades of astonishing and daring acts and travels to the most god-forsaken places in order to "give voice to those who did not have a voice,"[125] (as he himself, somewhat presumptuously, said) was also known to majorly re-write and re-create many events of his life in order to please those in power, his readers or maybe even himself.

Could we then still call his writing ethical journalism? Or is it simply a different literary genre? Kapuściński has been criticized again and again for insisting on calling his writing 'reporting' or 'journalism.' Jack Shafer writes,

> Every news story ever published could be better—contain a higher truth, if you will—if reporters were allowed to make up stuff. The measure of a journalist, especially a foreign correspondent, is to achieve the effect of Kapuściński without scattering the pixie dust of magical realism.[126]

In *Travels*, then, Kapuściński creates a completely new concept of an author and narrator for himself and re-tells his narrative of decades of serving the communist authorities while freely drifting between truth and fiction in his books. In *Travels* he lets go of the tyranny of narration and the superimposed layer of ideology and finally allows himself to enter an interesting form of an authorial self-critique, since over the years he gathers experience, wisdom and distance from

---

125 Ryszard Kapuściński, *Dałem głos ubogim...* (See Chapter 3, section II)
126 Shafer, "The Lies of Ryszard Kapuściński..."

reality. For years he strives to write something that he wants to see as ethical journalism while treating facts selectively and creatively – this effort results in a rupture. This rupture, in effect, turns out to be not damaging. On the contrary, it results in a new literary form of great literary value and significance, titled *Travels with Herodotus*.

Part Five
ETHICS

I. Ideological Ethics

In the preceding chapters I analyze *The Emperor, Imperium, Lapidaria* and *Travels with Herodotus*, discussing the author's approaches and attempts at shaping the world around him to fit his chosen narrative, and his process of gradually learning that the world actually shapes his narrative. Along with the transformation of Kapuściński's worldview and the passage of time, a noticeable shift in his writing method and formal writing approach becomes apparent: he relinquishes the narratorial grip, allowing his narrator to transform from a tyrant to a populist and affording room for an authorial self-critique.

Kapuściński slackens his narratorial grip slowly but surely. Over the years, he becomes less convinced about any one true and right ideology, growing increasingly experienced albeit embittered and loosening his narrator's grip over the narrative. In *The Emperor*, the narrator's control of the narrative is truly despotic, strangely but closely following the Ethiopian despot within the book's descriptions. In *Imperium*, the author's relationship with the Soviet Union/Russia, mainly from the inscribed valediction to the Soviet Union and to the communist system, garbles the shape of the narrative compared to the razor sharp delineation of the narrative in *The Emperor*. However, the most significant transformation is the new conception of a narrator in *Travels with Herodotus*. That narrator is someone outside of time and ideology; someone cognizant that no tyranny is eternal, even the tyranny of narrative. In *Travels with Herodotus*, the author is parting with despotism (even the narratorial one) and for the first time in his career allows for an interesting form of authorial self-critique through identifying himself with Herodotus, a historian and fictional storyteller.

I use the concept of interpretive tyranny similarly to Roland Barthes's conception of it outlined in *The Death of The Author*, Michel Foucault's famous definition of the notion of an author in "What is an Author?," and Erich Auerbach's explanation of biblical passages.[127] Henceforth, a text can be freed from interpretive tyranny only if it is detached from its author.

> We know that a text does not consist of a line of words, releasing a single "theological" meaning (the "message" of the Author-God), but is a space of many dimensions, in which are wedded and contested various kinds of writing, no one of which is original: the text is a tissue of citations, resulting from the thousand sources of culture.[128]

---

127 Erich Auerbach, *Mimesis: The Representation of Reality in Western Literature*, trans. by Willard R. Trask, Princeton: Princeton University Press, 1953.
128 Roland Barthes, *The Death of the Author*, ed. and trans. by Stephen Heath, New York: Hill and Wang, 1977.

In this renowned quotation, Roland Barthes postulates that a meaning of a literary text cannot and should not be reduced to the author's life and experiences. He famously announces the death of the author and through that detaches authority from authorship. A text – a "space of many dimensions" exists in a multilayered and multihued relation between all the elements that have gone and constantly go into its creation, as each text is "eternally written here and now."

Michel Foucault in his essay "What is an author?" states that an author is merely an author-function of a given work, and he or she exists only as a part of the text's structure but not of its interpretation.[129] Foucault warns of the dangers of looking during the process of interpretation for one "true" voice associated with the author. Instead, Foucault suggests, it is the language that should be seen as the "author" of a text.

It is a truism to say we do not exist for and by ourselves. We live with, because of, and through other people, and we are responsible for them. An irresponsible approach to facts from someone else's life is unethical, possibly leading to devastating results and perpetuating the vicious cycle of violence. Hence, the field of nonfiction, which deals with facts taken from real lives, is a territory where the writer's authority over truth is enormous and where truth should reign, but often does not. Kapuściński was highly conscious of this authority, and yet he recurrently abused it. His frequently selective handling of information, a somewhat nonchalant treatment of facts from other people's lives, a habitual re-invention of his own biography, a voluntary cooperation with the Polish Secret Police (Urząd Bezpieczeństwa, later Służba Bezpieczeństwa), and last but not least, his everlasting faith in the socialist ideology do not make the task of analyzing his books easy.

The master narrative of encountering "otherness" present in reportage books should compel the writer to employ an ethical approach to the described facts. Furthermore, creating a nonfiction narrative demands concurrent negotiation between the authorial vantage and the extratextual world, between the dry reality of facts and the creative act of writing. A reporter who decides to put his experiences in the form of a book faces a dilemma of negotiating between the ethical and aesthetical aspects of his work.

Adam Zachary Newton in *Narrative Ethics* analyzes the ethical consequences of narrating a story, and, as a result, fictionalizing the lives of the people enclosed by that narrative. Newton claims that every human relationship, including the reciprocal bonds between teller, listener, witness, and reader, is bound to be

---

[129] Michel Foucault, "What is an Author?," in: *Textual Strategies: Perspectives in Post-Structuralist Criticism*, edited by Jouse V. Harari, Ithaca, NY: Cornell University Press, 1979.

paradoxical: grasping someone's story means losing them as a real human being: "it is a way of appropriating or allegorizing that endangers both intimacy and ethical duty. At the same time, however, one's responsibility consists of responding to just this paradox."[130]

Implicit in Newton's clarification of the relationship between narrative and ethical obligation is Emmanuel Levinas' argument that consciousness and subjectivity can exist only if they are a result of an intersubjective encounter. Subjectivity is a responsibility toward an Other.[131] However, literature inevitably converts the interactive connections of ethics into aesthetic forms. Newton follows Levinas' line of thinking with a claim that literary texts fulfill their ethical function only if they "allegorize the crevasse dividing person from person, as well as the techniques they invent (for seeming) to traverse it."[132] An ethical nonfiction text is even a double challenge, as it has to invent techniques to "allegorize the crevasse" and simultaneously stay true to the facts.

The need to create narratives is timeless and does not depend on geography. Paul Ricoeur says, "To make up a plot is already to make the intelligible spring from the accidental, the universal from the singular."[133] Can an experiential moment be appropriated by literary tools? Does the author have the right to appropriate such a moment? Would that not be a totalizing act? An experiential appropriation inadvertently contains inherent violence, therefore in factual texts there should exist a constant tension between the author's need to tell a story and his anxiety that in doing so he may (mis)treat people and turn them into fictional characters, i.e. finalize their narratives. To rephrase: an author of a non-fiction book has to remain careful not to turn people into characters. Kapuściński's treatment of facts often does not heed Newton's advice. Kapuściński seems to not suffer from the anxiety of turning people into fictional characters, of finalizing their narratives. Even the title of the book containing his conversations with students *Dałem głos ubogim* ("I gave the poor a voice") inscribes itself into his rather arrogant presumption to "give the poor a voice," the basis of which is that their own voice was not good enough but had to be improved by Kapuściński. It would have been much more appropriate if he had entitled this book *Ubodzy dali mi głos* ("The poor gave me a voice"). The original title is just one of many

---

130 Adam Zachary Newton, *Narrative Ethics*, Cambridge: Harvard University Press, 1995, p. 19.
131 Emmanuel Levinas, *On Thinking of the Other: Entre nous*, translated by Michael B. Smith and Barbara Hershav, New York: Columbia University Press, 1991, p. 14.
132 Newton, *Narrative...*, p. 45.
133 Paul Ricoeur, *Time and Narrative*, translated by Kathleen McLaughlin and David Pellauer, Chicago: University of Chicago Press, 1984, p. 41.

examples of Kapuściński condescendingly appropriating the right to finalize the narratives of people he met and visited.

"Ethics are not just a problem of knowledge but a call to a relationship," says Gayatri Spivak, a long-term advocate for the rights of the Other.[134] The Other ought to be profoundly and responsibly engaged in a relation on equal, not exceptional, terms. Levinas, too, argues that an encounter between two people can be ethical only if each person recognizes the complete distinctiveness of the other. "Morality begins with the separateness of persons."[135] Thus it is crucial to not recreate the Other in the author's own image but allow him or her to create their own narrative, as "the object of ethical action is not an object of benevolence, for here responses flow from both sides."[136]

Kapuściński's approach to other people's narratives was not appropriately responsible or careful, even though he was convinced it was. It inscribed itself in Richard Rorty's explanation of a writer's indifference to suffering and failing to keep the ethical stance. In an article "The Barber of Kasbeam: Nabokov on Cruelty," Rorty, while mainly discussing Nabokov's own ethical stance toward his fictional characters and narrative, also talks about a general danger inherent in creating a narrative: "[an author] has to face up to the unpleasant fact that writers can obtain and produce ecstasy while failing to notice suffering, while being incurious about the people whose lives provide their material."[137]

The need to bear witness is at once horrible and at the same time disguised as honorable. Writing reportage is then a constant negotiation between the two aspects. Throughout his life, Kapuściński both reported and got involved in many wars and armed conflicts. Correspondents should not just report but also function as the world's vicarious conscience. It is not just a job; it is an obligation to deliver information to the world. Quite obviously, however, there is a gruesome facet of the correspondents' need to observe human suffering, which might make many people simply question the ethics of this job. Reporting from the hottest spots of the world, the sites of armed conflicts and wars requires a cautious weighing of facts in rendering the situation as judiciously as possible and not using it to promote oneself.

Many reportage books contain narratives of communities that are in some way disadvantaged, as those books are often written as a call to action for the

---

134 Gayatri Spivak, *The Spivak Reader: Selected Works of Gayatri Chakravorty Spivak*, ed. Donna Landry and Gerald MacLean, New York: Routledge, 1996, p. 24.
135 Levinas, *On Thinking*.... p. 309.
136 Spivak, *The Spivak Reader*..., p. 269-270.
137 Richard Rorty, *Contingency, Irony and Solidarity*, Cambridge: Cambridge University Press, p. 162.

general public. Frequently people described in such books cannot defend themselves, due to their disadvantaged position, be it politics, geography, tyrannical power, lack of education, lack of health, etc. Thus, an author who decides to interact with such communities and then write nonfiction books about their lives simply should attempt to stay true to what he or she had witnessed. It is, by no means, an easy task. A nonfiction writer is always caught in the dilemma of having to choose between truth and beauty. However, fulfilling this task (writing a good and convincing story while staying true to the facts) is not only possible but also noble.

Paweł Zajas, in an article, entitled "The Nature of an Ordinary Bug. A New Perspective on Non-Fiction Research," describes a referential pact between a reportage writer and his reader.[138] A referential pact denotes trust placed in the writer by the reader based on a premise that the writer, while creating a good story, stays true to the facts. Zajas claims that Kapuściński often, too often, broke that pact in his writing. Furthermore, Kapuściński did it consciously, not as a result of insufficient information or an impossibility to obtain the facts. He broke the referential pact while fully conscious of it. Zajas, in his otherwise excellent article, does not analyze Kapuściński's motivation for doing so. I, however, claim that Kapuściński's motivation for frequently deviating from the facts, often cutting them to desired shape, and conveying *his* version of the Third World to the First World, was that he assumed the peculiar role of a socialist missionary.[139] His justification for the breaking of the referential pact was a sacrifice of the facts on the altar of the Socialist Idea. Even though Kapuściński renounced the Communist Party membership, he never truly abandoned his socialist worldview. His socialist watchfulness for injustice, poverty, and discrimination as well as his burning need to divulge his findings with the world significantly limited his attempts at objectively cognizing the world. The ideological layer altered his picture of the world to a high degree. In Poland, it still remains a matter of heated discussion whether he was fully conscious of the ideological brackets his writing and worldview possessed. In my opinion, he believed in the socialist values so strongly for decades that he willingly turned a blind eye to all the atrocities and crimes the Soviet version of communism committed around the world.

The long list of Kapuściński's vices also has to include vanity, cockiness, his constant need to be praised, and escaping into easy generalizations. He felt great at a banquet in the brightest lime light, but at the same time he knew to strike up a conversation with the wait staff at that banquet. Throughout his care-

---

138 Paweł Zajas, *Teksty Drugie* 5, 2009: 40-55.
139 I thank Prof. Bożena Shallcross for this observation.

er he remained sensitive to the suffering of the disadvantaged and wrote about it without hypocrisy. He was very observant, curious to the point of annoyance, and as many claim – he was kind and friendly. It then stands to reason that Kapuściński was truly egalitarian in his views and had an acute sensitivity of unfairness and inequality. Whether it was a repercussion from the trauma of being ruthlessly uprooted and painfully poor in early childhood and having to witness the horrors of World War II or a life-long flirt with communism, or maybe all of the above, the end result is a fascinating combination of great prose and convoluted biography.

Zajas accurately remarks that postwar Polish reportage achieved such prominent status precisely because of having to avoid censorhip.[140] In no other article or book review have I seen a hint of understanding of the fact that Kapuściński was writing and working *against* a certain tradition. Even Adam Hochschild, who so wonderfully picked up the importance of Kapuściński's childhood trauma in the process of Kapuściński's worldview formation, did not take into consideration in his review of *Imperium* that trauma was only one of many elements shaping Kapuściński's worldview. On the other hand, Jack Shafer from *Slate Magazine* simply accused Kapuściński of being untrue and manufacturing or manipulating the facts. However, one has to remember that in pre-1989 Poland, Kapuściński, for many years, was writing against mainstream journalism. Pre-1989 mainstream journalism was labeled "objective" but in reality was subjective or even fictional, and it presented reality in such a way that benefited the system. Hence why Kapuściński's writing, subjective and biased in a sense, was actually welcomed in Poland. Ryszard Nycz deems Kapuściński's writing "antijournalistic" and through that definition he actually praises Kapuściński.[141] Reportage in Poland traditionally distanced itself from mainstream journalism, as mainstream journalistic texts were supposed to follow a formula created along the Party lines. Reading Kapuściński in the West is thus an example of a misunderstanding: Anglo-Saxon faithfulness to the facts versus the postwar Polish tradition of reading between the lines and alluding to or hiding the facts. Kapuściński's conviction of being on a socialist mission drove him to present the world in a way that was favorable to the system, yet the fact that he was brought up in a communist system taught him to simultaneously smuggle the illicit information into his writing. His upbringing and politics were inseparably tied to

---

140 Zajas, "The Nature…" p. 41.
141 Ryszard Nycz, *Tekstowy świat: poststrukturalizm a wiedza o literaturze*, Warszawa: Instytut Badań Literackich, 1995, p. 244. (translation my own) (See Chapter I Introduction, part 3, page 9)

the way his writing developed, and later, the passage of time and gathered experience also found their reflection in his writing.

In all of this deliberation and weighing of Kapuściński's vices and merits in the ethical treatment of the radical Other described in his books, one fact ought not escape our attention: reportage has to be based on the temporal and spatial immediacy of the writer to the witnessed facts. Therefore, the facts should be rendered in writing as close to the way they were witnessed as possible. Facts, therefore, have to remain 'rough,' or 'raw,' in order to preserve the veracity of the event.

Following Geoffrey Galt Harpham's view of correlations between language, literature, and ethics, we can arrive at an understanding of the role facts play in a narrative.[142] A fact or an image can be seen as an 'unbound energy,' as Freud would call it. Such energy needs to be 'bound' by a higher order (such as narrative), otherwise it will not pleasurably reduce tension; and that, according to Freud, is the goal of every individual. The author has to adjust his/her way of story-telling to enclose such an untamed image, or he will be forced to deal with the disorder the image imposes. Thus, "narrative ... is a form of repetition that is also a form of repression: gathered into a narrative, the individual image takes a subordinate and determined place within a structure that limits its anarchic potential to mean everything or nothing."[143] Formal coherence of narrative, then, represents order. However, images or facts defy the narrative order; they refuse to be narrativized. Such images are disconcerting precisely because they occur in narratives, especially in factual narratives, whose content can be verified in the outside world. And that verifiability makes such narratives threatening. The unrepressed horror of the rampant images resists narrative ordering and opposes closure.

Kapuściński gained international recognition in 1983, when the English language edition of *The Emperor* was published. Coinciding with this event was Kapuściński's decision to officially recant the membership of the Communist Party and turn his back on his previously reliable supporters – high ranking Party functionaries. *The Emperor* is a book in which the narrator exercises tremendous control over the narrative. As if in an attempt to mimic his own narrator and as if trying to control the rampant facts from his own life, Kapuściński 'fixes' his biography by shirking from his erstwhile loyalties and imposing a narrative order upon the facts.

---

142 Harpham, *Getting It Right: Language, Literature and Ethics*, Chicago: University of Chicago Press, 1992.
143 Ibid., p. 164.

In reportage, however, no narrative order or authorial skills ought to smoothen the edges of scratches made to the narrative surface by shocking facts. The facts remain shocking and they compromise the narrative order precisely because they are so shocking. Thus Kapuściński could not completely control the rampant facts, even though he made many (more or less successful) attempts at bending them. And in that lies the strength of nonfiction, this is where its call to action is located: nonfiction has to remain shocking, moving, it has to have to have rough edges and make the reader uncomfortable, otherwise the narrative will become a Disney movie.

The texts by themselves are incomplete; they become complete only by being read. Reportage texts not only make the reader ponder universal truths, but they become a call to action precisely because of their authenticity and factual basis. Reading them enables a sense of otherness that has a propensity for change, to make the reader examine and alter his or her own system of values. Consequently, in all accusations Kapuściński faces, the call to action and a propensity for change evoked in readers can actually be used to his defense.

Kapuściński tried to bend the narrative of the world according to his beliefs, but ultimately the world subdued his narrative. In other words, the transformation of his consciousness followed the process of differentiation in his writing and the search for a different formal method. The process resulted in a diversified oeuvre, out of which the reportage books remain the most interesting. They have already achieved the status of nonfiction classics, despite their author's many vices. They remain well written, captivating books with a great potential for alerting their readers to the problems of other nations and peoples.

II. Conclusion

While some critics may regard Kapuściński's works as representative of the fiction, rather than the nonfiction, genre, fact remains that ultimately his body of work belongs to the highest echelon of literature. Nonfiction constantly balances the questionable – presented as honorable – need to tell a story, and the often horrible – but genuine in its immediacy – act of bearing witness. In other words, nonfiction unremittingly demands consideration of both the ethical and aesthetical aspects of a factual story. The vacillation, incessant balancing act, and downright necessity to attain the golden medium between ethics and aesthetics are integral for nonfiction: they secure constant public interest, evoke an inherent dialectical tension that does not allow them to ossify and contain immutable and incontrovertible truths.

The elements I analyze – that of Kapuściński's life events assuming the form of books, of the ideological base upon which he rests his conception of the world, of tailoring factual events to impart a preconceived intent, of even fabricating the facts as well as his own perpetually contrived and controlled public image – have not dissuaded me from being a proponent of Kapuściński. During the course of writing this study, my interpretation and relationship with his books seemed to shift in stages: complete acceptance eventually became total aversion, finally arriving at placable, indulgent approval. The trajectory of my focus does not overlap with the rekindling of interest and reevaluation of Kapuściński's works prompted by his death (which did not occur simultaneously with my own writing process) evident in Poland and around the world. Most importantly, this reconsideration had been deferred until his death to save the author any shame or pain. Only the final sections of my work coincide with recent critical revelations about Kapuściński.

As mentioned before, reportage writing is a constant balancing act between aesthetics and ethics. Tracing Kapuściński's steps in this book and exploring his own vision of writing, I have focused on the aesthetic aspect of his works in order to arrive at the conclusion that the ethics actually plays a much larger role. Kapuściński himself often considered the aesthetic element: the structure of his own penmanship, the sheer difficulty of writing, and the need to wrench sentences out of himself. Having analyzed his works, I arrive at the conclusion that regardless of his own statements, the most salient feature of his writing is an ethical one. His ethics derives from socialist values, learned and internalized during his activist youth, guiding Kapuściński through his adventures and books. As I mention above, his socialist sensitivity to injustice, poverty, and discrimination may have impeded his cognitive tasks, but nevertheless his impetus was genuine and motivated by a true egalitarianism. He has often been criticized that aside from his literary treatment of poverty and injustice, he personally did very little to combat these issues. I disagree. His books have spurred multitudes of people to be sensitive to these flagrant problems. Kapuściński's true egalitarianism becomes apparent when considering his influence in propagating interest in the far corners of the world. Moreover, his sensitivity to suffering and his attunement to the human condition have reached thousands, perhaps millions of his readers around the world.

Precisely due to their questionable factual basis and the subsequent, jarring ethical clash, his books remain examples of literary mastery. Most importantly, Kapuściński's works constantly incite discussion and consideration of the fundamental aspect of the mission undertaken by today's literature and mass media – the issue of epistemological responsibility.

Works cited

Althusser, Louis. "Ideology and Ideological State Apparatuses." *Lenin and Philosophy*. Translated by B. Brewster. New York and London: New Left Books, 1971.

Auerbach, Erich *Mimesis: The Representation of Reality in Western Literature*. Translated by Willard R. Trask. Princeton: Princeton University Press, 1953.

Bakhtin, Mikhail. *The Dialogic Imagination*. Translated Caryl Emerson and Michael Holquist, Austin: University of Texas Press, 1981.

Barthes, Roland. *The Death of the Author*. Edited and translated by Stephen Heath. New York: Hill and Wang, 1977.

Beauchamp, Tom L. and James F. Childress. *Principles of Biomedical Ethics*. New York: Oxford University Press, 2001.

Bereś, Witold and Krzysztof Burnetko. *Kapuściński: nie ogarniam świata*. Warszawa: Świat książki, 2007.

Berlin, Isaiah. "The Bent Twig: A Note on Nationalism." *Foreign Affairs* 51 (Oct 1972): 11-30.

Bissel, Tom. "On the Road with History's Father." *New York Times*, June 10, 2007.

Bruss, Elisabeth. *Autobiographical Acts: The Changing Situation of a Literary Genre*. Baltimore: John Hopkins University Press, 1976.

Burke, Jason. "Beyond the Spectacle." Internet article available at: http://www.literaryreview.co.uk/burke_06_07.html

Caruth, Cathy. "Unclaimed Experience: Trauma and the Possibility of History." *Yale French Studies* 79 (1991): 181-92.

Clifford, James.

> "On Ethnographic Authority." In *The Predicament of Culture: Twentieth-Century Ethnography, Literature and Art*. Cambridge: Harvard University Press, 1988.
>
> George E. Marcus, eds. "Introduction: Partial Truths." In *Writing Culture: The Poetics and Politics of Ethnography*. Berkeley: University of California Press, 1986.

Code, Lorraine. *Epistemic Responsibility*. University Press of New England, London, 1987.

Cohen, T. and Guyer P. *Essays in Kant's Aesthetics*. Chicago: University of Chicago Press, 1982.

Couser, G. Thomas.
- *Altered Egos*. New York: Oxford University Press, 1989.
- *Vulnerable Subjects: Ethics and Life Writing*, Ithaca and London: Cornell University Press, 2004.

Curry, Jane Leftwich, ed. *Poland's Journalists: Professionalism and Politics.* Cambridge: Cambridge University Press, 1990.

Domosławski, Artur. *Kapuściński: Non-fiction*. Warszawa: Świat książki, 2010.

Foley, Barbara. *Telling the Truth: The Theory and Practice of Documentary Fiction.* Ithaca and London: Cornell University Press, 1986.

Foucault, Michel.
- "Des Escapes Autres." *Architecture/Mouvement/Continuité*. Paris: October 1984.
- "What is an Author?" In *Textual Strategies: Perspectives in Post-Structuralist Criticism*, edited by Jouse V. Harari.. Ithaca, NY: Cornell University Press, 1979.

Freud, Sigmund. *The Interpretations of Dreams*. Translated by Joyce Crick, with an introduction and notes by Ritchie Robertson. Oxford: Oxford University Press, 1999.

Frus, Phyllis. *The Politics and Poetics of Journalistic Narrative: The Timely and the Timeless.* Cambridge: Cambridge University Press, 1994.

Frye, Northrop. *The Anatomy of Criticism: Four Essays*. Princeton: Princeton University Press, 1957.

Genette, Gérard. "Vraisemblance et motivation." *Communications* 11, 1968.

Głowiński, Michał. *Gry powieściowe. Szkice z teorii i historii form naracyjnych.* Warszawa: Państwowe Wydawnictwa Naukowe, 1973.

Hamlin, Garland. [1894] 1960. *Crumbling Idols*. Reprint, Cambridge: Harvard University Press.

Harpham, Geoffrey Galt.
- "Imagining the Centre." In *Critical Ethics: Text, Theory and Responsibility*, edited by Dominic Rainsford and Tim Woods. New York: St. Martin's Press, 1999.
- *Getting It Right: Language, Literature and Ethics*. Chicago: University of Chicago Press, 1992.

Harris, Joseph. "The Plural Text/The Plural Self: Roland Barthes and William Cole." In *College English* 49, No. 2 (February 1987): 158:170.

Hart, Francis R. "Notes for an Anatomy of Modern Autobiography." *New Literary History* 1, No. 3 (1970): 485-511.

Hartsock, John C. "'Literary Journalism' as an Epistemological Moving Object Within a Larger 'Quantum' Narrative." In *Journal of Communication Inquiry* 23:4 (October 1999): 432-446.

Heidegger, Martin. *Being and Time*. New York: Harper, 1962.

Heisenberg, Werner. *Physics and Philosophy: The Revolution in Modern Science*. New York: Harper and Row, 1958.

Hemingway, Ernest. *For Whom the Bell Tolls*, New York: Scribner, 1940.

Hochschild, Adam. "Magic Journalism," *New York Review of Books* 41:18 (Nov. 1994).

Ingarden, Roman "On So-called 'Truth' in Literature." Jean G. Harrell and Alina Wierzbiańska, ed. *Aesthetics in twentieth-century Poland: selected essays*. Translated by Adam Czerniawski. Lewisburg, Pa., Bucknell University Press, 1973.

Jarzębski, Jerzy. "Między 'realizmem' a 'prawdą': proza krajowa po wojnie." *W Polsce czyli wszędzie*. Kraków: Wydawnictwo Zielona Sowa, 2000.

Kapuściński, Ryszard.

Another Day of Life. Translated from the Polish by William R. Brand, New York: Vintage International, 2001.

Autoportret reportera. Kraków: Wydawnictwo Znak, 2003.

Dałem głos ubogim: rozmowy z młodzieżą. Kraków: Wydawnictwo Znak, 2008.

The Emperor: Downfall of an Autocrat. Translated from the Polish by William R. Brand, Katarzyna Mroczkowska-Brand. New York, London: Harcourt Brace Jovanovich, 1982.

Imperium. Translated from the Polish by Klara Glowczewska. New York: A. A. Knopf, 1994.

Lapidaria. Warsaw: Czytelnik, 1990-2007.

"Marzenia naiwne." *Dziś i jutro* 6, 1950.

Notes. Warszawa: Czytelnik, 2005.

O książkach, ludziach i sztuce. Warszawa: Czytelnik, 2009.

"Pisane szybkością." *Dziś i jutro* 32, 1949.

Prawa Natury. Kraków: Wydawnictwo Literackie, 2006.

"Rozmowy na ulicy." *Sztandar Młodych* 7, 1957.

Rwący nurt historii: Zapiski o XX i XXI wieku. Kraków: Wydawnictwo Znak, 2007.

Shadow of the Sun. Translated from the Polish by Klara Glowczewska. New York: Vintage, 2001.

Shah of Shahs. Translated from the Polish by William R. Brand, Katarzyna Mroczkowska-Brand, San Diego: Harcourt Brace, Jovanovich, 1985.

Ten Inny. Kraków: Wydawnictwo Znak, 2006.

"To też jest prawda o Nowej Hucie." *Sztandar Młodych* 234, 1955.

Travels with Herodotus. Translated from the Polish by Klara Glowczewska. New York: A. A. Knopf, 2007.

"Wielki rzut." *Polityka* 5, 1950.

Kinston, Maxine Hong. *The Woman Warrior*. New York: Vintage, 1977.

Kurzyna, Mieczysław. *Wańkowicz*. Warszawa: Authors Agency, 1972.

Langer, L. L. *Holocaust Testimonies: The Ruins of Memory*, New Haven, CT: Yale University Press, 1999, p. 77.

Lacan, Jacques. *Ecrits. A Selection*. Translated by A. Sheridan. New York: Norton, 1977.

Legvold, Robert. Review of *Imperium*. *Foreign Affairs* 73: 6 (1994): 178.

Levinas, Emmanuel. *On Thinking of the Other. Entre Nous*. Translated by Michael B. Smith and Barbara Harshav. New York: Columbia UP, 1991.

Lyotard, Jean Francois. *The Postmodern Condition: A Report on Knowledge*. Minneapolis: University of Minnesota Press, 1984.

de Man, Paul. *The Rhetoric of Romanticism*. New York: Columbia University Press, 1984.

Mickiewicz, Adam. "Powrót taty." *Ballady i romanse*. Vilnius, 1822.

Miłosz, Czesław. *Nobel Lecture*. New York: Farrar Straus Giroux, 1981.

Nałkowska, Zofia.

Ściany świata. Warszawa: Gebethner i Wolf, 1931.

Medaliony, Warszawa: Czytelnik, 1946; *Medallions*, English translation by Diana Kuprel, Evanston, IL: Northwestern University Press, 2000.

Nelson, William K. *Fact or Fiction: The Dilemma of the Renaissance Storyteller*. Cambridge: Harvard University Press, 1973.

Newton, Andrew. *Narrative Ethics*. Cambridge: Harvard University Press, 1995.

Nietzsche, Friedrich. [1873] "On Truth and Falsity in Their Ultramoral Sense." *Early Greek Philosophy & Other Essays*. Translated by M. Mugge. Vol. 2 of *The Complete Works of Friedrich Nietzsche*. New York: Russel & Russel, 1964.

Nowacka, Beata and Zygmunt Ziątek, *Ryszard Kapuściński: Biografia pisarza*, Kraków: Wydawnictwo Znak, 2008.

Nycz, Ryszard. *Tekstowy świat: poststrukturalizm a wiedza o literaturze*. Warszawa: Instytut Badań Literackich 1995.

Pipes, Richard. "Is Russia Still an Enemy?" *Foreign Affairs* 76:5 (Sept-Oct 1997): 73.

Plato. *The Republic and Other Works*. Translated by B. Jowett, New York: Anchor Books/Doubleday, 1973.

"Point of View: The Newspaper and Fiction." *Scribner's Magazine* 40 (1906): 122-24.

Reisner, Steven Psychic. "Trauma and the Seductions of a Painful Past." *Studies in Gender and Sexuality* 4:3 (2003): 263-286.

Ricoeur, Paul. *Time and Narrative*. Translated by Kathleen McLaughlin and David Pellauer. Chicago: University of Chicago Press, 1984.

Rorty, Richard. *Contingency, Irony and Solidarity*. Cambridge: Cambridge University Press, 1989.

de Saussure, Ferdinand. *Writings in General Linguistics*. Oxford: Oxford University Press, 2006.

Scholes, Robert. *Structural Fabulation: An Essay on the Fiction of the Future*. Notre Dame: University of Notre Dame Press, 1975.

Shafer, Jack. "The Lies of Ryszard Kapuściński, or, if you prefer, the "magical realism" of the now-departed master." *Slate Magazine*, Jan. 25, 2007.

Shelley, Percy Bysshe. "Ozymandias." 1818.

Spivak, Gayatri. *The Spivak Reader: Selected Works of Gayatri Chakravorty Spivak*, ed. Donna Landry and Gerald MacLean. New York: Routledge, 1996.

Suetonius, Tranquillus Gaius. *The Twelves Ceasars*. New York: Penguin, 2000.

Tejumola, Olaniyan. "Narrativizing Postcoloniality: Responsibilities." *Public Culture* 5:1 (Fall 1992): 50.

Tighe, Carl. "Ryszard Kapuściński and *The Emperor*." *The Modern Language Review* 91: 4 (Oct 1996): 927.

Tolstoy, Leo. *War and Peace*. Translated by Rosemary Edmonds. Harmondsworth, Middlesex: Penguin Books, 1968.

Torańska, Teresa. *Them: Stalin's Polish Puppets*. New York: Harper and Row, 1987.

Wagner, Roy. *The Invention of Culture*. Chicago: The University of Chicago Press, 1981.

Waldstein, Maxim K. "Observing *Imperium*: A Postcolonial Reading of Ryszard Kapuściński's Account of Soviet and Post-Soviet Russia." *Social Identities* 8: 3 (2002): 481-499.

Ważyk, Adam. "Poemat dla dorosłych." *Nowa Kultura*. (Aug 1955), No. 34.

Wedeen, Lisa. *Ambiguities of Domination: Politics, Rhetoric, and Symbols in Contemporary Syria*. Chicago: University of Chicago Press, 1999.

Wimsatt, William K. & Brooks, Cleanth. *Literary Criticism: A Short History*. New York: Knopf, 1957.

Wolny-Zmorzyński, Kazimierz.

Sztuka reportażu wojennego Melchiora Wańkowicza, Rzeszów: Wydawnictwo Wyższej Szkoły Pedagogicznej w Rzeszowie, 1991.

Reportaż: wybór tekstów z teorii gatunku. Rzeszów: Wydawnictwo WSP w Rzeszowie, 1992.

Zajas, Paweł.

"Lost Cosmonauts: On Ryszard Kapuściński's *Imperium* and Its Critics – Once More." *Teksty Drugie* (3: 2010): 218-231.

"The Nature of an Ordinary Bug. A New Perspective on Non-Fiction Research." *Teksty Drugie* 5, 2009: 40-55.

Zavarzadeh, Mas'ud. *The Mythopoeic Reality: The Postwar American Nonfiction Novel*. Urbana: University of Illinois Press, 1976.

Ziątek, Zygmunt. *Wiek dokumentu: Inspiracje dokumentarne w polskiej prozie współczesnej*. Warszawa: Instytut Badań Literackich, 1999.

Ziółkowska, Magdalena, *Blisko Wańkowicza*, Kraków: Wydawnictwo Literackie, 1975.

Žižek, Slavoj. *The Sublime Object of Ideology*, London, New York: Verso, 1999.

Polish Studies – Transdisciplinary Perspectives

Edited by Krzysztof Zajas and Jaroslaw Fazan

Vol. 1 Artur Płaczkiewicz: Miron Białoszewski: Radical Quest beyond Dualisms. 2012.

Vol. 2 Kinga Kosmala: Ryszard Kapuściński: Reportage and Ethics or Fading Tyranny of the Narrative. 2012.

www.peterlang.de

Artur Płaczkiewicz

Miron Białoszewski: Radical Quest Beyond Dualisms

Frankfurt am Main, Berlin, Bern, Bruxelles, New York, Oxford, Warszawa, Wien, 2012. 193 pp.
Polish Studies – Transdisciplinary Perspectives. Vol. 1
Edited by Krzysztof Zajas and Jaroslaw Fazan
ISBN 978-3-631-61873-8 · hb. € 39,80*

Miron Białoszewski: Radical Quest Beyond Dualisms is an innovative and challenging work of literary scholarship that examines Białoszewski's artistic praxis as a certain philosophical proposition. It differs from the earlier critical approaches to the writings of this writer in as much as it attempts to examine his mature poetry from a non-dualistic perspective. The study demonstrates in detail how Białoszewski's radical approach to poetry evolves into a consistent life-writing and life-philosophy (life-writing-philosophy). The poet disregards binary oppositions and he approaches life and reality without any universal method. In the poet's mature poetry, the context is identified as life and not as reality, and Białoszewski's writing is described as his life project which is not searching but rather researching, since it has no pre-established goal to reach except for being continued.

Content: Non-Dualistic · Postmodern · Nonjudgemental · Antihierarchical · Postmodernism · Neo-Pragmatist · Life-Writing · Life-Philosophy · Anti-essentialist · Beyond Representation or Traversing Platonic Split · Beyond Visual Reality or Traversing Cartesian Split · Beyond Metaphysics or Traversing Kantian Split · Slavic Studies · Polish Poetry · Comparative Literature · Deleuze · Rorty

*The e-price includes German tax rate. Prices are subject to change without notice

Frankfurt am Main · Berlin · Bern · Bruxelles · New York · Oxford · Wien
Distribution: Verlag Peter Lang AG
Moosstr. 1, CH-2542 Pieterlen
Telefax 00 41 (0) 32/376 17 27
E-Mail info@peterlang.com

40 Years of Academic Publishing
Homepage http://www.peterlang.com